*f*P

The Free Press

New York   London   Toronto   Sydney   Singapore

The Music of Light

The Extraordinary Story of

Hikari and Kenzaburo Oe

Lindsley Cameron

*f*P

THE FREE PRESS
A Division of Simon & Schuster Inc.
1230 Avenue of the Americas
New York, NY 10020

THE FREE PRESS and colophon are trademarks
of Simon & Schuster Inc.

Designed by Carla Bolte

Manufactured in the United States of America

10 9 8 7 6 5 4 3 2 1

Library of Congress Cataloging-in-Publication Data

Cameron, Lindsley.
    The music of light: the extraordinary story of Hikari and
Kenzaburo Oe/Lindsley Cameron.
    Includes bibliography, discography, and index.
    1. Ōe, Hikari, 1963–   . 2. Composers—Japan—Biography.
3. Savants (Savant syndrome)—Japan—Biography. 4. Ōe, Kenzaburō,
1935–   . I. Title.
ML410.038C36 1998
780'.92—dc21
    [B]   97–49506
                                                              CIP
                                                               MN
ISBN 0–684–82409–4

To Kenzaburo, Yukari, and Hikari Oe

with boundless admiration

Contents

Acknowledgments

Portions of this book have appeared, in different forms, in *The New Yorker, The New York Times, The Yale Review,* and *The Japan Society Newsletter.*

For various kinds of assistance, I would like to thank:

Dr. Jamshed Bharucha; John Finlay; David Fratkin; Eiko Fukuda; Ann Goldstein; Julie Gray; Peter Grilli; Alexandra Horowitz; Juzo Itami; Jamie James; Professor Donald Keene; Anita Keire; Philip Kennicott; Christopher Kidd; Yoshiko Kuwahara; Paula Lawrence; Ann Martin; Daniel Marx; Dr. Leon Miller; Naoyuki Miura; Bruce Nichols; Mary Norris; Hikari, Kenzaburo, Sakurao, and Yukari Oe; James R. Oestreich; Mari Ono; Seiji Ozawa; David Remnick; Dr. Seth Roberts; Alex Ross; Megumi Sasaki; Martha Serrille; Charlotte Sheedy; Kirk Stirling; Dr. Darold Treffert; and Yoshiaki Yamato.

Preface

The book you are about to read is the story of someone who is absolutely unique. Not only unique, but unique in more than one way. Hikari Oe was born with two brains, one alive and one dead. The dead one was in a growth on his skull, a growth so large that he appeared two-headed. The operation that removed it left him with severe developmental disabilities, yet he grew up to be such a successful composer that CD sales of his works have consistently broken records for living composers in the classical category, now totaling $8 million worldwide.

He is unique in scientific terms, in the particular way his achievements have surpassed his limitations. He is not the only developmentally disabled person who has had a successful artistic career, but he is the only developmentally disabled person who has had a successful career as a composer. He is also the only developmentally disabled person who composes without performing; others have improvised in the course of performances, but he is the only one who creates music in his head and notates it directly, without using an instrument. In this way he is, so far as anyone knows, the only one of his kind in human history. Apart from his medical singularity, he is also unique in the way that every creative artist with a distinctive voice is, of course—but for that matter (until someone begins cloning us) every human being is unique, and so is every snowflake.

But Hikari Oe is also unique in another way, one that eludes scientific measurement: he is a member of a unique—and uniquely creative—family relationship. And his story is therefore necessarily the story of the other member of that relationship, too. His father, the novelist Kenzaburo Oe, winner of the Nobel Prize in Literature in 1994, has made unique—and uniquely constructive—use of him. Hikari has figured in his father's fiction in a fascinating variety of ways ever since he was born, when he inspired a novel that is widely regarded as one of the greatest of this century. So far as I know, there has never been a literary relationship like that of Kenzaburo and Hikari Oe.

Hikari's importance to his father cannot be overstated. In a speech given at the International Conference on Rehabilitative Medicine in Tokyo, in 1988, Kenzaburo Oe acknowledged that "the central theme of my work, throughout much of my career, has been the way my family has managed to live with this handicapped child. Indeed, I would have to admit that the very ideas that I hold about this society and the world at large—my thoughts, even, about whatever there might be that transcends our limited reality—are based on and learned through living with him."

In their personal, family relationship, they are so intertwined that it would be impossible to tell Hikari's story without Kenzaburo's. Observers close to the family have marveled at the extent and the nature of their interdependence; Dr. Nobuo Moriyasu, the surgeon who performed the operation that saved Hikari's life when he was a baby, wrote in his diary in 1983, "I have been treating Hikari for twenty years, but I can't say that I really understand the full extent of Oe's feelings for his son. Still, in reading a number of his novels and critical works, I've gradually come to realize that what he experiences in his relationship with Hikari has a lot in common with the feelings of a doctor for his patients." In fact, Hikari and his father are mutually dependent in a way and to a degree that would be unusual anywhere, but is all the more so in Japan.

Oyako is Japanese for mother and child. A single word: their relationship is seen to be so close—and so indissoluble—that they are even united linguistically. *Oyako* is what Japanese family life is built around, what it's there to serve. It is, strikingly, a closer bond than it is in the West. Babies may spend much of the first three years of their lives being carried on their mother's backs even today, and Japanese women often help school-age children in ways that Western mothers would not extend beyond infancy: cutting their food for them, even helping boys to urinate. It is generally assumed in Japan that one's relationship with one's mother is the closest and warmest that one will ever know; mothers are expected to offer a lifelong unconditional love that no one really expects to find in a romance or a marriage. And this works two ways: the love a woman feels for her children is considered a dependable source of fulfillment in a way that marriage is not. Japan has no equivalent of the traditions of courtly love that led to idealized expectations of romantic happiness through marriage in the West: in Japan, arranged marriages were the rule well into this century, and are still common.

When Hikari Oe was born, working mothers were virtually unheard of; the society operated under the assumption that being a mother was a full-time job. And, indeed, it was all but impossible for a woman a few years beyond marriageable age to get a job—or even keep one—retirement being expected of women at around age twenty-six. The situation has changed a bit since then, but working mothers are still a rarity. And customs, laws, and public opinion as embodied in multifarious forms of popular culture see the protection of the nurturing mother and her child or children as society's most essential goal.

The father-and-child bond is given comparatively short shrift; it's more a matter of stern Confucian duties and head-of-the-family responsibilities. In the West, a father who went out drinking with his colleagues every night after work, staying out so late that his children were in bed before he came home, would be regarded as a bad parent. In Japan, such a man is considered a good father: drinking with his colleagues is expected of him, actually a duty; shirking it would almost certainly cut off opportunities for professional advancement and therefore be a betrayal of his most important responsibility as a parent, which is ensuring the security of his wife and children. A father in America who turned down a corporate posting because it would entail a long separation from his wife and children would not be thought unreasonable, and a wife who persuaded him to turn it down would be acting understandably; in Japan, the husband's decision would scarcely be regarded as sane, and a wife who persuaded him to make it would be seen as extremely selfish and immature.

Kenzaburo Oe's close, and in some ways quasi-maternal, relationship with his son, who is mentally stuck forever in childhood and its dependency, has an element of rebellious originality, a quality that permeates Oe's writing, his political stances and gestures, his jokes, and even his helping out at home with shopping and cooking (rare for Japanese men even now, and especially unusual for one of his generation)—virtually every aspect of his life, in fact. By the time Hikari was thirteen, he wrote, "The birth of the handicapped first baby in my real life has continuously influenced my fictional world long after the composition of 'A Personal Matter.' If I had not existed in this real world, my son would not be here. But, on the other hand, if he were not here, I could not be living the way I am. At the time of his birth . . . in the midst of confusion and commotion, as I almost prepared both birth and death certificates, I let my instinct have its way and named the boy Hikari [light]. My instinct was right. His existence has since illuminated the dark, deep folds of my consciousness as well as its bright sides."

He wrote a number of stories and novels using characters who shared some of Hikari's attributes. Oe scholars call them the "Idiot-son Narratives." By 1981, the "idiot sons" had recurred so often in Oe's fiction that the Oe scholar and translator Michiko Niikuni Wilson published an essay about them called "Oe's Obsessive Metaphor," and Oe has written more idiot-son narratives since then. The social critic Takashi Tachibana (best known for discovering and publicizing the corruption that brought down Prime Minister Kakuei Tanaka, in 1974) said, "Without Hikari there would be no Oe literature."

The process of creating fiction is often misunderstood. Routinely, journalists breezily inform their readers that a fictional character "is" some actual person. Novelists' biographers, even when they describe a character as being "based on" or "inspired by" some real person, may then go on to use a quotation from the work the character appears in as evidence for the novelist's feelings about the real-life human being on whom the character was based.

This is misleading, to say the least, but in some cases the novelists themselves may bear some responsibility for the confusion. Kenzaburo Oe has created many characters who resemble Hikari. Several of them are called Mori, one is called Jin, and others are called—Hikari. Furthermore, the ones called Hikari have fathers who are famous writers, and who share many attributes with Kenzaburo. Most of the Hikari-like characters are nicknamed Eeyore, after the ludicrously pessimistic donkey in A. A. Milne's children's books, and Hikari's real-life nickname is Pooh, after the pudgy, dim-witted teddy bear in the same series.

Now, it is hard enough to explain to people who have never written fiction themselves that a character who resembles a real-life person must not be confused with his or her real-life model. When the borrowed attributes include the real-life model's actual name, readers cannot really be blamed for losing track of the distinction between created fiction and inspiring fact. And in a way, the persistence of such confusions is testimony to the strength of the created work: art, in its tidy, pruned coherence, is more satisfying than the random mess of daily life. It is meant to be.

But if authors are exasperated by the public's failure to see their fictions for the creations they are, that is understandable, too. By the time Hikari was nineteen, Kenzaburo's attempts to explain the difference between his son and his Hikari-like characters had taken on an almost desperate tone. In an essay, he said, "I have written a lot about the physical abnormality of my child and his retardation. However, I have not done so in the manner of the 'I-novel.'" The I-novel (*shishosetsu* or *watakushishosetsu*) is a Japanese literary genre. I-novels are, basically, fictionalized memoirs, confessional narratives; when Kenzaburo says he has not written about Hikari in that manner, he is emphasizing that he has not put his experiences with his son into his novels as though he were writing a factual memoir but has consciously transformed aspects of his son's life and condition into something else.

His essay continues, "I am the father of a brain-damaged child, and I have written stories about him, but I have not presented him as I would in an 'I-novel.' . . . His existence in real life continues to make various kinds of impacts on me. To live in this world, for me, is to live with him. What these impacts had produced, what was at the core of our communal life—only when these things became *imaginatively independent* and came out of my interiority, did I write about him.

"I live in this cosmos-world-society as a human being. This child of mine deeply and sharply influences the structure of my flesh and spirit. Therefore, when I write about trees and whales, these words, which embody symbolic meanings, constantly reflect the shadow of the child's existence. Conversely, I write about the idiot infant. The words that describe him, however, do not portray the retarded child who exists in my own family. My words . . . like a surrealist painting that places the sky and an ocean in the orifices of a human body, are the *very image of this cosmos-world-society* which I glimpse through the flesh and spirit of my idiot child."

Unsurprisingly, statements like that one appear to have done nothing to clarify the distinction in the popular mind. As late as 1994, in the press coverage that followed the Nobel award, reporters felt free, in print and on television, to quote dialogue spoken by characters in Oe novels as though they were quoting something the author himself had said in an interview.

Generally, if an author creates a character who resembles a real-life person very closely, the real-life person can tell the world that he or she is separate from the character. In this country, someone who feels damaged by being confused with a fictional avatar can even sue. A woman is suing Joe Klein and his publisher right now because she claims her colleagues have mistaken her for a character in *Primary Colors*. The situation is different when the voice someone is given as a character is the only voice the person has. Hikari Oe's ability to use language is limited. He does have a voice of his own, but it is a voice that expresses itself in music, not in speech. Hikari can't use it to say explicitly that he isn't one—or any—of the "idiot sons" in his father's books.

And the fact that the man who has given him literary life gave him biological life as well complicates matters further. Parents usually control the ways their children are presented, at least while the children are still *children*—ignorant, helpless, and dependent.

Apart from the self-consciously literary presentation of Hikari through characters like him, his father has sometimes presented a kind of distilled, literary version of the story of Hikari's beginning to speak. In saying this, I am not saying that Kenzaburo has told lies. On the contrary, he focused on an important and critical moment in the course of Hikari's painful and erratic progress toward human communication; artist and shaper of stories that he is, he cleared away details that seemed too trivial or irrelevant to include. "In my writing, I never lie about my son," he said in a 1992 interview for the *Tokyo News*. "I write what Hikari says after putting it in order." His rearrangements are not made with any deliberate intention of falsifying; indeed, he has always exerted himself to tell what he felt was the real story, excluding whatever he felt might get in its way.

I have sometimes wondered whether if Hikari had never existed, Kenzaburo would have found it necessary to invent him. There is a kind of mythic Hikari who existed long before the actual person named Hikari Oe was even conceived. In an essay in a Japanese magazine, Kenzaburo Oe wrote, "When I was groping my way along as a novice writer, I repeatedly characterized the child/infant as an 'abandoned foundling.' . . . As long as he was born out of the unconscious, he was delivered into this world as if he were a plaything. If that is the case, he might also be destroyed like a plaything." World mythology and folklore apart, Kenzaburo Oe was writing about this archetype—a child society wants to destroy because it is defective—as early as 1958, five years before Hikari's birth, in his first novel, *Nip the Buds, Shoot the Kids*. Some reform-school kids have been evacuated, in the last days of World War II, to a remote rural village. The headman, who is in charge of them, shows the reader what a bad guy he is by telling one of them, "Listen, we should strangle a bastard like you while you're still a kid. We crush cripples while they're babies. We're peasants, we nip the buds that won't grow. . . . We can push you off the cliff, we can kill you and nobody'll accuse us of murder." Oe has described that novel as an account "not factual but mental" of his experiences as a child during World War II. Similarly, some of his accounts of Hikari are "not factual but mental": true in imaginative and emotional ways.

The theme of the baby who is rejected as defective appears again in a later novel, *The Game of Contemporaneity,* written when Hikari was sixteen. This book uses local legends from the remote rural region where Kenzaburo Oe spent his childhood. It includes an alteration to the Japanese creation myth: the World Parents Izanagi and Izanami, the founders of the Japanese race, give birth to a legless baby, Hiruko. The infant is abandoned because of this deformity, cast adrift in a reed boat. Eventually, Hiruko shows some heroic qualities.

In *M/T and the Marvels of the Forest,* written six years later, Kenzaburo Oe uses the folklore of his childhood again, presenting it more straightforwardly. And there are consonances with the literal facts of Hikari's story in the local legends here, too: a hero's cranial scar, for example, is associated with his extraordinary powers, just as Hikari's unusual cerebral configuration is, in medical terms, part of what makes his achievements possible. Hikari himself—as himself, more or less—appears in this narrative. What Hikari does and says is partly true, partly invented. One of his musical compositions—a piece the real Hikari actually wrote, which was inspired by this folklore—figures in the story, and the score of this piece was included in the published book.

Hikari's successful commercial career as a composer began with that publication of that score. Kenzaburo sent Hikari's own voice into the world, and the world listened and wanted to hear it again and again.

In recent years, Hikari's growing and increasingly independent fame as a composer has meant that Kenzaburo is no longer his only public spokesperson. At home and in private life, Hikari's mother, brother, and sister have acted as his interpreters, along with his father, and continue to do so. And his music teachers and the performers who have worked with him can voice his views about his music as no one in his family has been able to do.

Public versions of Hikari Oe have proliferated outside the musical community, too, and his public persona has steadily acquired new shapers. An hour-long, award-winning Japanese television documentary about Hikari and his father reached an enormous audience, creating a definitive image of the pair for many people whose notions of who they were had been fairly vague. In this country, a half-hour segment of a widely seen news program presented Kenzaburo more as Hikari's father than as an important figure in his own right. Most of the people who saw it were probably hearing of both Oes for the first time. And in both programs, while Hikari himself is shown, and recorded speaking, the authentic voice of his music, used extensively in the soundtrack, lets him speak directly to the audience in the one medium of communication that he has mastered perfectly.

In addition, Hikari's uncle Juzo Itami, the director of many internationally successful films (*A Taxing Woman,* for example), made a movie version of Kenzaburo's novel *A Quiet Life,* one of the works of fiction where Hikari appears, under his own name, as a character. It was released in Japan, and an English-language version has been prepared but had not yet been sold as of the time this book went to press. The Hikari Oe in Itami's movie is composed of various Hikaris: the character his father created, who includes his father's perceptions and memories of his real-life son, is augmented by his uncle's perceptions and memories of his real-life nephew. But in the movie, again, Hikari's music on the soundtrack lets Hikari communicate directly with the audience and present himself to his listeners through the medium in which he expresses himself best. At the same time, of course, they are receiving an image of the composer that has been created partly by his father, partly by his uncle, and partly by the actor who plays his role.

This book adds yet another portrait of Hikari to the gallery. In writing about him, I have sometimes felt like someone copying a picture from a reproduction. My opportunities of meeting the original were very limited, his ability to communicate is circumscribed, he is painfully shy and seems really at ease only in speaking to members of his family or people he knows very well. And the story I am telling here is not only the story of the real-life Hikari, the man and the composer, but also the story of the versions of Hikari that have gone out into the world, chiefly through his father's writing.

Like a myth, Hikari Oe's story lends itself to many tellings. Indeed, Hikari has actually lived out a tale that is encountered in myth and folklore all over the world. In a musical context, Hikari might be compared to the operatic Siegfried, who gains treasure and love through his hard-won ability to understand what a bird tells him, or to another Wagnerian hero, Parsifal, the "pure fool" whose innocence confers healing power and enables him to attain the Grail that has eluded older and wiser knights. But because his story is being told in a book, the most important element in it is absent, for the real Hikari Oe is most truly and completely expressed in his music. And it is, finally, his music that in an unimpeachably objective, scientific sense makes him unique.

This book attempts to explain how it is possible, in light of all we understand currently about the workings of the human brain, for Hikari to do what he has done in spite of his limitations. But since no one else with similar limitations has ever composed music as Hikari has, the resemblances between Hikari and others who have shown musical brilliance of various kinds despite similar limitations go only so far. And so we are left with a mystery, something that can be explained, in a way, yet not really understood.

Two factors were almost certainly crucial to his unprecedented creative accomplishments: the genes he inherited and the loving, imaginative, and constructive way he was raised. But if it is possible for someone with Hikari's disabilities to compose music, why hasn't anyone else with similar disabilities ever done it? We do not and cannot know. And Hikari's achievements remind us of the limitations of our knowledge. We should be grateful for the reminder, for it is such a hopeful one. Anything we regard as impossible, individually or collectively, is impossible only until it happens; so our range of possibilities is always greater than we know.

Author's Note

Before beginning Hikari's story, I would like to say something about why and how I came to tell it. The first novel Hikari inspired his father to write was *A Personal Matter*. My own interest in the Oes began when I read it, in 1969, the year it first came out in English. I stayed up all night to finish it and actually sobbed in relief when, in the final pages, the young father who is its hero decides to save the life of his defective baby instead of allowing it to die. I also laughed aloud, often, while reading other scenes. I have since learned, from talking to others who have read it, that my reactions were not uncommon, for it is a remarkably powerful book.

But I had personal reasons for such strong emotion. I myself had been an unwanted child, thrown away by my parents and given up for adoption. And my adoptive parents had later adopted another little girl from the same agency where they had obtained me. They gave her my original name—Alexandra, the name that had been on my birth certificate. When she did not develop normally and was diagnosed as having cerebral palsy, they simply sent her back to the adoption agency as though she were a piece of defective merchandise being returned to a department store.

Why am I telling you all this? First, to acknowledge that while I have done my professional best as a journalist in collecting and presenting information about Hikari Oe, I cannot claim to have produced an entirely objective account. Because of these early experiences, I could not do so; my feelings about the issues involved in his story are too strong, my identification with him too intense and too complicated. My response to both Kenzaburo's work and Hikari's was also undeniably affected by this personal history, and my readers have a right to know that the critical judgments expressed in this book are not the product of a coolly detached sensibility. Second, to say that the same experiences that precluded objectivity were also what made it possible for me to tell the story at all. They prepared me to be a particularly receptive reader of Kenzaburo Oe, what with his repeated use of the themes of abandoned children, defective children, and children who are abandoned or killed—or who narrowly escape being abandoned or killed—because they are defective. I read all the Oe that was translated into English, as soon as it came out, and when Hikari's CDs were released here, in 1995, I was assigned to write about the composer for the *New York Times* because of my familiarity with his story through his father's work, which I had also written about for the *New Yorker.*

I first met Kenzaburo Oe that spring, when he came to New York in connection with publicity for the English-language publication of *Nip the Buds, Shoot the Kids*. He had been interviewed by many American journalists after the Nobel award, but most had read little of his work. Pleased and touched to find a sincere and deeply responsive fan among them, he graciously extended our scheduled interview by several hours.

It turned out to be the first of many interviews he generously gave me over the course of two years; these were my most important source for this book. I met Hikari and Yukari, too, when they joined Kenzaburo in Princeton in the fall of 1996; the family not only invited me to spend an entire day with them but fed and entertained me very kindly while I pestered them with questions far into the night. And since the bulk of my information about all the Oes came from interviews and correspondence with them, the reader should assume that these were the source of any quotation not otherwise identified.

I must add something about the ways I have referred to the Oes. Partly because of their unfailingly exemplary courtesy, but also because writing about any Japanese people makes one morbidly conscious of polite usage, I find myself wincing when I write about the Oes as Kenzaburo and Hikari, as though they were both children. Writing about the novelist in articles and reviews, I call him Oe, using his children's personal names if I mention them.

Hikari the composer should by rights be called Oe, too. But since his career is so closely interwoven with his father's writings about him, and since, moreover, much of my information about Hikari comes from his father, I soon discovered that any attempt to refer to these two Oes as anything but Kenzaburo and Hikari led to absurdly tangled sentences. So I have called them by their personal names here, most of the time. I have referred to Kenzaburo's wife as Yukari so she will not be confused with his mother, and simply followed suit in referring to Hikari's brother and sister. I trust it is clear that in doing so, I have meant no disrespect.

And since you are going to be seeing a lot of these names in the pages that follow, you might like to know how they sound (approximately, at least). Oe is pronounced like the letters *O* and *A:* OH-eh; Kenzaburo as KEN-ZAH-buh-roh; Hikari as hee-KA-ree. Hikari's mother is Yukari (you-KAH-ree); his sister is Natsumiko (nat-SOO-mee-koh); his brother, Sakurao (sa-KOO-raoh).

"Monster Baby"

On June 13, 1963, in Tokyo, Kenzaburo and Yukari Oe, one of the most glamorous couples in Japan, had a very unusual baby, their first child. A world-famous figure now, Kenzaburo, at twenty-eight, was one of his country's most famous writers; even at such an early age, he had already been famous for years.

He had come from the boondocks—from the remote south-western island of Shikoku. He was born and grew up in a village so tiny that it was eventually legislated out of existence. The Oes were a good family, prosperous small landowners who came down in the world as a result of the postwar land reforms. Kenzaburo's father had been in charge of an operation that pulped tree bark for the Japanese government to use in printing paper money. He was in some ways a rather mysterious figure, revealing little to his children about earlier phases of his life, when he had traveled in China and perhaps in other countries, too; he knew several foreign languages. He had died when Kenzaburo was nine, and Kenzaburo's mother has been either unable or unwilling to tell him much about the father he never had a chance to know as an adult. Kenzaburo's emotions about the father he lost so early—and about whom he had so frustratingly little information—found their way into his fiction eventually and were also undoubtedly a strong factor in his own approach to fatherhood. His wife also lost her father at an early age; this must have been a source not only of the couple's closeness to each other but also of the depth of their determined involvement with their children.

Kenzaburo's mother was set on finding educational opportunities for her talented son. "I was a very vulnerable boy in my village," Kenzaburo would later say, "very weak, speaking strangely, and always thinking and reading many books. My mother protected me, and she was determined that I should escape." Today, Kenzaburo is plainly grateful to his mother, and their relationship is obviously an affectionate one, yet he tells many stories about his mother's wry putdowns of his literary achievements. He understands that she is teasing him, but at the same time, he says, "she is sincere." His own style of humor is often gleefully self-deprecatory, but when he talks in that vein about his mother, one senses a wistfulness under the impish enjoyment. He spent the difficult years of his late boyhood having been abandoned by his father—through death—with a mother who was loving and protective, but who tended not to express her affection with direct warmth; these factors surely affected his own style of parenthood.

In high school, Kenzaburo found a friend who seems to have provided some compensation for what was missing at home: a big, tough, savvy kid called Ikeuchi, who decided to take Kenzaburo under his wing. Under the name Juzo Itami, this friend went on to become a movie star and is now one of Japan's most famous directors, with such international hits as *A Taxing Woman*. His father had been a director, screenwriter, and essayist; using the stage name Mansaku Itami, he was a key figure in the early development of Japanese cinema. Kenzaburo says today that meeting Juzo Itami "was the start of all my happiness," for besides ensuring his survival among the high-school bullies, Juzo introduced him to his lovely younger sister, Yukari, whom Kenzaburo later married. The first time he saw her, she was doing some chore in the yard when he had gone to the Ikeuchis' house with her brother. She could never remember that occasion, but Kenzaburo could never forget it: "It was always that way with me and pretty girls," he says.

Kenzaburo's older brother worked to finance Kenzaburo's studies at Tokyo University, the most prestigious and competitive in the country. Kenzaburo was a highly promising student, majoring in French literature, but it was the fiction he wrote while still an undergraduate that brought him his early fame. "The Catch," a short story, won the Akutagawa Prize, one of Japan's top literary awards, and is now considered a classic. It has an oddly prophetic moment; a black American airman is held prisoner in a remote Japanese village, guarded by the local children, including the narrator. When the American takes the boy hostage, grabbing him by the throat and threatening to strangle him if the adults come any closer, the boy's father can save his son's life only by maiming him, crushing the child's hand with the hatchet he uses to kill the soldier. Five years after writing it, Kenzaburo would face a similar decision about saving his own son's life.

Kenzaburo married Yukari Ikeuchi in 1960. She was not only

beautiful but artistically gifted. Within a year of their marriage, the talented young couple were facing extraordinary trials. A fearlessly rebellious writer in a time of intense political turmoil in Japanese history, Kenzaburo was often in the news. In 1961, a highly controversial story, "Seventeen," concerning an actual event in the previous year—the assassination of the chairman of the Socialist Party by a rightist youth of that age—had infuriated conservatives. They wanted to think of the assassin as an idealistic, heroic figure, but Oe's unsparing portrait shows a pathetic kid, not quite sane, in a society that offers nothing to shore up his weaknesses.

"Seventeen" had provoked death threats and other nerve-wracking forms of harassment from right-wing extremists—thugs bellowing insults in front of the Oes' house, rocks thrown through the windows of Kenzaburo's study, constant menacing, middle-of-the-night phone calls. The publisher of the magazine in which the story appeared, terrified in the wake of an assassination attempt (by another seventeen-year-old rightist) on another liberal publisher, which left his wife wounded and a maid dead, printed a public apology for having published Oe's story. Because Oe did not disassociate himself from this apology, angry leftists began attacking him, too, accusing him of cowardice.

Kenzaburo Oe could have had a successful career as a scholar, but he chose to be a creative writer instead. And his writing enraged his enemies and alienated his friends. He felt that he had made the wrong choice, but that it was too late to resume an academic career. Oe wrote later that he spent the years from 1961 to 1963 falling deeper and deeper into a suicidal funk. Speaking of these years, he told an American journalist, "I continued to write, but my work was not so good. I was thinking of giving up writing novels."

When Yukari learned that she was pregnant in 1962, Kenzaburo and she had every reason to hope that the birth of their first child might pull him out of his slump of self-doubt, giving him a

4

new sense of purpose, and of hope. During her pregnancy, Kenzaburo wrote a two-part novella that sheds some light on his state of mind at the time. Its title—literally, *Sexual Humans*—is difficult to translate and has sometimes been rendered *Homo Sexualis,* sometimes *Perverts.* When an English-language edition finally came out in 1996, it was called *J,* after its main character. The last half of this novella is a masterpiece, but while it is exhilarating to read, it could have been written only by a deeply disillusioned—and perhaps only by a deeply despairing—man. J is the spoiled young son of a steel magnate. J's first wife has killed herself. His father's money having rendered J immune to the usual social constraints, he leads a dissolute life, of which the novella's opening, describing an orgiastic weekend in the country with his second wife and their friends, gives an example. But the dissipations that his wealth makes possible do not move him, and in the second part of the story, he has surrendered to a compulsion to molest women on public transportation. His only emotional connections are with two fellow molesters. One of them is a young poet who justifies his crimes with a highfalutin philosophy; the other is a distinguished old man, evidently of very high social standing.

Although J has been responsible for a good deal of human wreckage, he is given an all-is-forgiven chance to redeem himself—to let his unhappy, unfaithful wife marry the lover who has made her pregnant and to begin working for his father's company like a responsible bourgeois citizen. And he appears to be taking that chance, but at the last moment he rushes down into the nearest subway entrance and, rejecting the hypocrisy such a life would entail, molests a woman in such a way that he must be—and is—caught.

J can be read as an allegory about freedom, and about man—Everyman—in society. But it lends itself to a more personal reading, too. "I write with my genitals," Oe once said in an interview, in response to critics who had complained about his sexual explicitness. He now regards that statement as thoughtless, superficial, and immature—nothing but a young man's expression of anger—yet it is worth examining in this context. In the story, the sexual impulse can be seen as standing for a writer's creative urge—exhilarating in itself, and utterly irresponsible. But its author understands that the urge to self-expression, if not curbed by conscience, is a fundamentally antisocial thing. In "Seventeen," following an artist's kind of conscience to represent a young terrorist honestly, he had transgressed against another kind of conscience, subjecting his young wife to predictable threats of violence and other kinds of attacks. In *J*, Kenzaburo Oe was—at least on some level—examining questions about the selfishness of the creative artist, questions he would continue to explore in later fiction, and questions that the birth of his first baby made searingly important.

For the baby, a male, was born a monster. With its brains spilling out of its skull, it looked as if it had two heads.

The diagnosis was encephalocele, or brain hernia, and the prognosis was grim. The Oes were presented with the cruelest kind of dilemma. Doctors told them that if their baby did not have surgery, it would die. If it did have surgery, though, it would be a "human vegetable," incapable of even the most basic functioning. In any case, the doctors themselves could not decide at once whether to operate; they had to wait to determine how much living brain tissue was contained in the sac protruding from the hole in the baby's skull. If there was a significant amount of it, removal of the growth would simply end the infant's life.

Just after Hikari was born, Kenzaburo was offered a journalistic assignment: to go to Hiroshima to report on an international nuclear-disarmament rally, the Ninth World Conference against Atomic and Hydrogen Bombs. It gave him an opportunity to flee from the agonizing decision he was facing in Tokyo. He has written of experiencing "the intense feeling that the problem of my child would suffocate me if I couldn't get out into a larger arena, see things from a broader perspective." Leaving his infant son lying in a hospital incubator, liable to die at any moment, Kenzaburo accepted the assignment.

He later wrote that he had never "experienced so exhausting, depressing, and suffocating a journey." He left the oppressive heat of Tokyo for the even more stifling southern city, accompanied by a magazine editor whose first daughter had just died. (The editor would later become the head of Iwanami, which published many of Oe's books.) The travelers had yet another cause for mourning, too; a mutual friend had just hanged himself in Paris.

And the conference was a debacle, ruined by factionalism and disorganization. "Each time I get near the Peace Park," he wrote, "I smell the strong odor of politics." Disgusted by the way the lofty—and humanistically imperative—aims of the participants had so easily been scuttled by their human weaknesses, Kenzaburo Oe began devoting more and more of his attention to the A-bomb victims in the city and to the doctors who worked with them.

He met Dr. Fumio Shigeto, the director of the Hiroshima A-Bomb Hospital, in the early days of the conference. Oe has often written about the effects of this meeting, which were profound. Although stressing that he is not a religious man, he finds himself using religious words like "conversion." Dr. Shigeto had arrived in Hiroshima to start work as a vice president at the Red Cross Hospital only a week before the bomb fell. On the day of the explosion, he ran from the train station, neglecting the head wound he had suffered in the blast, to the hospital, stopping only to render medical aid to others along the way. For months afterward, camping out in the blasted city, sleeping minimally, working in a hospital fetid with the stench of the rotting corpses piled up outside, he devoted himself to relieving the sufferings of the bomb victims—and remained on call for the survivors for decades. Having some expertise in radiology, he was among the first in Japan to understand the consequences of the nuclear explosion: he first suspected the nature of the bomb—and the long-term destructive consequences of its radioactivity—when he noticed that the hermetically sealed Xray film stored in the hospital and the ordinary camera film he was trying to use to document the bomb victims' injuries could not be used, having been exposed by the bomb's radiation.

Oe has written several accounts of a young colleague of Shigeto's. Despite the fractures and burns he had sustained in the explosion, he joined in the medical relief work just after the bomb was dropped. This young doctor asked Dr. Shigeto why the people of Hiroshima would have to go on suffering even after the war had ended. Frustrated by the inadequacy of anything he could do for the bomb victims, who were rapidly dying or irreparably damaged, the young doctor hanged himself from a bolt sticking out of a broken wall half an hour after asking his despairing question.

Oe found the suicide natural enough, given what the young man had endured and seen, and what he feared. And Oe was overwhelmed by the courage of Dr. Shigeto and others like him, who, as he has written again and again, did not commit suicide although they had every reason to: "A handful of doctors, some of them injured and all surrounded by a city full of casualties, had the brute courage to care for over a hundred thousand injured people with only oil and mercurochrome."

And the doctors were not the only heroes Oe found in Hiroshima. He was impressed by the courage of the bomb victims, left handicapped, disfigured, diseased, dying—yet struggling on, making the best of their situations, and in some cases altruistically devoting themselves to relieving other victims or exerting themselves in the cause of nuclear disarmament, so that future generations should not suffer what they had suffered.

The only personal revelation Oe makes in *Hiroshima Notes,* his book of reportage about this journey, is his confession of a childhood obsession that never quite went away. He had gone to see a movie with his father, and in the film a captured soldier committed suicide to make sure he would not reveal any military secrets. Kenzaburo was afraid that he himself was the kind of person who would never chose death over dishonor. Disingenuously, he asked his father why the soldier had killed himself, and his father told him brusquely that the soldier would have been killed anyway, after having been forced to tell whatever he knew. And young Kenzaburo began from that moment to feel an even worse fear—the fear that he would be the kind of person who would chose dishonor over death but get death anyway, death in shame and disgrace.

He offers this reminiscence to introduce a discussion of the concepts of "dignity," "humiliation," and "shame," explaining that as a student he had often been struck by how often these words occurred in French literature but how relatively rare their equivalents were—and how comparatively little force they had—in Japanese. "I saw things related to the worst sort of humiliation in Hiroshima," he writes, "but for the first time in my life I saw there the most dignified Japanese people."

Traditionally, Japan has segregated the handicapped. Kenzaburo knew that if his son survived, he could expect little in the way of support from the society around him, and that the parents of a handicapped child would be criticized for nurturing it lovingly.

Names are very important to Kenzaburo. He has chosen all his children's names with care, the names of the characters in his books often have very complex resonances, and he enjoys discussing such things as the possibly prophetic significance of his grandmother's being named Fude, which means the kind of brush traditionally used for writing in Japan. He named his first son Hikari, which means "light."

"After he was born, when the doctor told me he couldn't see, I wanted to give him sight," Kenzaburo says, "and since I couldn't do that, I wanted at least to give him a name related to sight. I was reading Simone Weil at the time, and in one of her last works there is a long letter about a legend in Inuit folklore. They say that at the beginning of the world there was no light, and there were no human beings, only crows. And the black crows had to get their food off the black ground. One day one of the crows said, 'If only there were light, it would be so much easier for us to live.' And God heard the crow, and created light. For Simone Weil, the important point of the story was that if we pray for something intensively, our prayer will be granted. So, thinking of this story, I asked my mother whether she thought it would be better to call my son Karasu [crow] or Hikari [light]. She knew I really intended to call him Hikari, and had suggested Karasu only playfully, so she recommended Karasu just to tease me." He might not have been permitted to do so; the Japanese government can prevent parents from giving their children names it doesn't approve of. And even if it had been allowed, a bizarre name would have subjected the child to a lot of teasing. "So I called my son Light." (Hikari seems unable to escape the name he was almost given, though: the occupational training center he attends every day is called Karasuyama [Crow Mountain], and the character for "crow" is a variant of the character for "bird"—one stroke is missing—as it appears in the school he graduated from, the Seicho [Bluebird] School for the Handicapped.)

"But at the time I couldn't know the real significance of the name I had given him. He has truly become the light of my family, and in the light of my son, I can continue my work.

"He was born in the year the Shinkansen"—the ultrafast "bullet train"—"was introduced, and one of the Shinkansen trains was called Hikari, because light moves so fast. So we sometimes tell people, for a joke, that he was named after the train, and that I wanted to call my other son Kodama [the name of another train]."

Kenzaburo happened to be in Hiroshima in the middle of August, when the Japanese festival of the dead is celebrated. One of the customs associated with the festival is writing the names of the dead—family members, friends, mentors—on lanterns that are floated on streams, lakes, and oceans. Kenzaburo joined some others who were doing this, and realized that he had unthinkingly written his son's name on the lantern he had launched. Unconsciously, he seemed to perceive the child as something not alive.

"I didn't hesitate at all," Kenzaburo said many years later, in a television interview. "My Hikari was still alive, but I felt that he was dead. So I wrote the name of Hikari on a lantern and set it afloat. My lifelong friend Yasue lost a daughter, and he wrote her name on a lantern. I think he didn't like the idea of my writing Hikari's name, but I sent off the lantern anyway. Yet after I did it, I thought about how I was treating my child as if he were dead, even though he was still alive, and I felt that this was the most destructive thing I could do to myself. You know, setting a lantern afloat for that child was really sentimental. Then I hated myself, that evening, going back in the twilight. . . . I still remember how I hated myself. My child had suffered a major accident at birth, and I didn't have the courage or the willpower or the upright sort of heart needed to accept him and handle it with him."

Kenzaburo's Hiroshima experiences led him to decide to authorize the problematic surgery that was his newborn son's only hope of living. Dr. Shigeto had told his young colleague, "Right in front of our eyes, people are suffering. What can we do except use all our strength to treat them?"

In the same television interview, Kenzaburo also said, "Dr. Shigeto told me that he should have talked more to that young doctor, but I felt that he was referring to me. Right before my eyes, my son was suffering. What could I do except use all my strength to save him?" There was a good chance that the surgery itself might kill the baby, but if it did, at least his parents would know they had done all they could to save their child's life. If not, though, they faced the grimmest of possibilities. The doctors told them that the most probable result of an operation would be to produce a vegetable—an utterly dependent, scarcely human being, virtually comatose, perhaps incapable even of moving, requiring exhausting and expensive twenty-four-hour care for a lifetime and giving nothing whatsoever in return. "I never thought of actually killing my baby," Kenzaburo says now, "but I did dream, in a confused way, that he might simply die, that this burden would just be lifted from us."

Assuming the responsibility for producing such a being, something neither clearly dead nor fully alive—and making the commitment to care for such a child—would have been a courageous decision in any country, at any time. But in Japan in 1963, it took incredible guts, flying in the face of centuries-old traditions in a rigidly conservative society where the personal consequences of bucking tradition were among the gravest in the world.

The bravery of this young father's decision can be understood only by examining the history of Japanese attitudes to the handicapped. The two main sources of the difference between Western accommodation and Japanese intolerance are Shinto—the ancient, indigenous Japanese religion—and Buddhism. The two creeds are not mutually exclusive, and Japanese people today, even if they consider themselves atheists, can hardly get through life without participating in some of the ceremonies (Shinto weddings, for example, and Buddhist funerals)—and certainly find their attitudes influenced by the beliefs—of each.

Shinto ceremonies revolve largely around the concept of purification, of ridding the participants of pollution. The referee of a sumo match, for example, purifies the wrestlers by sprinkling salt in the ring before the contest begins. When Western readers see the words "purification" and "pollution" in a religious context, they tend to think the pollution must be moral. But in Shinto it is not; it is physical. Shinto's dirt is not the metaphorical dirt of sin and guilt that Western religion addresses; it is just plain old dirt. And from the earliest moments of Japanese recorded history, sickness, death, and contact with the sick, including the wounded, and with the dead and dying were considered polluting.

Buddhist beliefs—widely accepted in Japan for the past thousand years—introduced another factor into Japanese attitudes to physical afflictions. According to Buddhist doctrines, sufferings in the life of any given human being may be the result of his or her misdeeds in previous incarnations. The parents of a handicapped baby, for example, though they—as their present selves—have done nothing to deserve their burden, may be expiating the sins they committed as other people, in past lives, and their handicapped child, too, may be paying a karmic debt incurred in a previous existence. At best, such beliefs may make it easier for people to resign themselves to life's crueler blows; at worst, though, especially when the beliefs linger unconsciously in a vestigial way—not as beliefs but as unexamined assumptions—they can justify the kind of heartlessness that comes under the heading of "blaming the victim."

There is another factor in Japanese attitudes toward the kind of problem the Oes faced in deciding what to do about their baby boy. This is Confucianism, which is not really a religion at all but a moral philosophy, deeply ingrained in all east Asian culture. Its relevant aspect here is the conception of a dependent child as its parents' absolute property. There is a custom in Japan called "family suicide": most typically, a father directs his wife to kill their children, then kills her, then kills himself. Such things happen in the West, too, but rarely; there's no one word in English for this act. It's not a common occurrence in Japan now, either, but it has been happening regularly there for hundreds of years, and there's a word for it in Japanese. The idea that justifies it is that of being responsible for, rather than to, one's dependents. If you're going to stop providing for them (by killing yourself), you owe it to society to prevent anyone else's being burdened with the obligation you're abandoning.

And there is one more factor that should be stressed in explaining the Oes' predicament. Kenzaburo and Yukari, and the doctors who were treating their baby, were well-educated people who had grown up at a time when it was obvious to everyone that the resources of their country were being strained to the maximum. No thoughtful person who had lived through the famines at the end of the war, or who had endured the years of privation that followed the defeat, could be unaware that the amount of time, money, talent, and medical expertise required by an individual with no apparent productive potential could be seen as a sort of wanton sin against rationality. This was 1963; Japan's economic miracle had not yet begun. If Hikari were to live, he could be seen as doing so only at the expense of others—others whose lives were more likely to justify the commitment of scarce resources.

But Kenzaburo says that his wife never hesitated for a moment over the decision to give Hikari the operation that offered his only chance of life and that she was determined from the start to devote herself to raising him. Both the baby's grandfathers were dead. His grandmothers were supportive. Kenzaburo's mother was a re-markably independent-minded woman, and from the beginning she was determined to do whatever she could to promote her grandson's welfare. Living in far-off Shikoku, her immediate re-sponse to the news of Hikari's problematic condition was to spend several hours praying for the baby's survival at a shrine she main-tained to a local god. Yukari's mother came to help. Today, Ken-zaburo and Yukari maintain an endearing one-upmanship over whose mother loved Hikari more. Yukari talks about how *her* mother appreciated Hikari's being a well-behaved and placid child when he was small; Kenzaburo says *his* mother "admired Hikari just for existing."

Other relatives strongly criticized the young couple—how could they even consider taking extraordinary measures to avoid a death that was so clearly desirable? An aunt of Kenzaburo's, his mother's sister, refused even to visit the baby, although she lived in Tokyo and would in normal circumstances have hurried to the hos-pital, proud and excited to be the first in her family to see her suc-cessful nephew's first-born son. But Kenzaburo and Yukari were not deterred; the operation was authorized after Kenzaburo re-turned from Hiroshima, when Hikari was ten weeks old.

Though the difficult decision had finally been made, it could not be implemented instantly. There was a nerve-racking waiting period while doctors ascertained whether the surgery was feasible; they had to monitor the lump growing out of the hole in the baby's skull to be sure it could be detached safely. Although Kenzaburo's mother hated leaving her native valley, she, too, came to Tokyo to help.

On the night before the operation, Kenzaburo pointed out to his wife and mother, as they comforted each other in the baby's hospital room, that being born in such grim times might not necessarily be a good thing. But they ignored him. And Kenzaburo's mother told Yukari of legends from her part of Shikoku about the dead being revived on hearing the voice of a family member.

When Hikari was being prepped for the operation, a barber whose shop was near the hospital had been brought in to shave his head. But after shaving the front part of the baby's cranium, he was dismayed when he felt the soft, spongy texture of the growth in the back of the skull; he refused to proceed, saying he didn't want to take the responsibility, the task was beyond his skill. Hikari's grandmother, who had been sitting shyly in a corner of the room, asked him to give her the razor. Referring to Shikoku traditions, she muttered scornfully that he wouldn't have had the mettle to participate in a peasants' revolt, and finished shaving Hikari's head herself.

Dr. Nobuo Moriyasu, one of Japan's top brain surgeons, performed the operation, removing the growth and covering the hole in the cranium it had protruded from by affixing a plastic plate to the baby's skull. While Hikari remained in the pediatric intensive-care ward, until November, Dr. Moriyasu supervised his treatment. Typical complications associated with surgery for cranial encephalocele include developmental delay, mental retardation, seizures, and visual problems; all of these arose in Hikari's case.

Kenzaburo's mother returned to Shikoku after the operation but continued to do her bit for her grandson. While his surgical wounds were healing, she prayed for his recovery by lighting candles on the family altar in front of a statue of a nineteenth-century local hero, credited with magical powers, who, like Hikari, had a scar on the back of his head.

Kenzaburo grappled with his experience in his usual constructive way—he wrote about it. Indeed, he produced the novel that many critics still regard as his greatest. *A Personal Matter* was published when Hikari was one year old. It was phenomenally successful, first in Japan, then, as it came to be translated (into English, Dutch, French, German, Spanish, Norwegian, and Swedish), in countries all over the world. It is about a young father called Bird whose wife has just given birth to a "monster baby"—a child with a condition exactly like Hikari's. It is a work of fiction, not by any means a straightforward account of Oe's own experiences, yet it plainly conveys the anguish involved in deciding what to do about such a child. In one scene, for example, an obstetrician tells the father, "If I may be frank, I think the baby would be better off dead, and so would you and your wife. Some people have a funny way of being optimistic about this kind of case, but it seems to me that the quicker the infant dies, the better for all concerned."

Bird is no saint and no hero, and his states of mind are revealed with a stunning honesty that is probably the strongest factor in the book's success. He's a cram-school instructor with a wistful dream of going to Africa. When the book opens, his wife is still in labor, and he is distressed at the realization that parenthood will put an end to his irresponsible youth, cutting off the chance of such adventures. Once his son is born and he learns of the baby's problematic condition, he hopes the boy will simply die before his parents are called upon to make any decisions about it at all. Conspiring with his mother-in-law to keep his wife in ignorance, he is disappointed, then terrified as the infant grows and thrives. He comes to see it as an enemy: "The baby continued to live, and it was oppressing Bird, even beginning to attack him." Yet he identifies with it increasingly, even while he escapes his responsibilities through drink and sex, staying with an unconventional former girlfriend from his college days. He loses his job and, with his lover, plots to kill the obstinately enduring baby (by taking it to an abortionist who will feed it nothing but sugar water until it is dead) and escape to Africa after all.

But in the end he can't go through with it. "What was he trying to protect from that monster of a baby that he must run so hard and so shamelessly?" Bird asks himself. "What was it in himself he was so frantic to defend? The answer was horrifying—nothing! Zero!" And he dashes off to save his baby, although his lover does her best to dissuade him. The baby survives the operation, and it turns out that brain hernia was a misdiagnosis. Yet the story leaves the baby's fate unclear: he may develop normally, or he may be severely retarded. In either case, Bird is determined to pull himself together and get a job that will enable him to provide for his child.

Like "Seventeen" and *J, A Personal Matter* demonstrates Oe's remarkable ability to make his readers see—and feel—all they have in common with seemingly unsympathetic characters. Bird's temptation is understandable, and, chiefly because Oe has shown a likable, intelligent, and fundamentally decent person while recording all his basest impulses with unsparing honesty, by the end of the book readers come to identify with Bird and to care deeply about what he will do. There is no sentimentality whatsoever in this novel, and it is made clear that the commitment to a "vegetable baby" would destroy Bird's freedom forever, yet it is also clear that killing the baby will destroy everything about Bird that would make his freedom worth having.

It's a profoundly serious book, but much of its success must be due to its sheer entertainingness. Where it is funny, it is very funny indeed. Japanese society, as embodied in Bird's employers, his students, his mother-in-law, and the hospital bureaucracy, comes to function almost like a cartoon villain, constantly popping up in different disguises. And Bird is a comic character himself, most gloriously so when he has what is surely the most hilarious hangover in all of world literature. (Yes, even funnier than the hangover in

Kingsley Amis's *Lucky Jim*. Aficionados of the comic novel might like to know that Kenzaburo had been reading Amis at around the time Hikari was born.) The "monster baby," too, seems at times a brilliantly grotesque representation of nothing less—and nothing more—than life itself, simple biological life. But the book's most striking quality is its utterly unsparing honesty, the quality that many critics have singled out as the one aspect of Kenzaburo Oe's work that most sets him apart from other writers.

A Personal Matter was not the only work Hikari's condition inspired during the first year of his life. Before it came out, Kenzaburo had published a story, "Aghwee the Sky Monster," which is also about the father of a baby with a brain hernia. The story is in some ways a mirror image of the novel. The father—a young composer—has killed the baby while its mother was comatose, starving it to death by giving it only sugar water. And the murdered baby—called Aghwee, after the only sound it ever made—appearing to him as a monstrously large infant in the sky, in the end kills the father, too. It is an ambiguous narrative; like *The Turn of the Screw,* it offers readers the option of interpreting it as a ghost story or as an account of a disturbed personality. But in either case, the father's narcissism proves fatal, whether the apparition is seen as having an actual existence or as a hallucination caused by a guilt too great to bear.

Many of the novels and short stories Oe has gone on to write since *A Personal Matter* have made it particularly difficult to determine where fact ends and fiction begins. He has created characters based in the most obvious ways on himself and members of his family, sometimes even giving these characters the names of their real-life inspirers. In several ways, his family's privacy was sacrificed to his writing career.

In 1967, when Hikari was four and his sister, Natsumiko, was born, Kenzaburo Oe published his next major novel, *The Silent Cry,* which proved highly successful in Japan and abroad. It is still regarded as one of his most important works. The novel tells the story of two brothers from Shikoku. The older brother is the father of a baby with a condition much like Hikari's: "The baby gazed up at me with wide-open eyes, but whether he was hungry or thirsty or felt some other discomfort I couldn't tell. He lay with eyes open and expressionless, like a marine plant in the water of the dusk, simply and placidly existing. He demanded nothing, expressed absolutely no emotion. He didn't even cry. One might wonder if he were alive at all."

This child has been placed in an institution. The baby's mother has become an alcoholic, in part owing to depression over the birth of this defective child. This brother had left Shikoku long ago to complete his education in Tokyo, but the younger stayed behind with their retarded sister and their mother, who was not quite sane. By the time Kenzaburo wrote this novel, Hikari had begun to show some interest in sounds and music, if in almost nothing else, and this interest is evidently what inspired Kenzaburo to imagine something almost spookily prophetic. The brother says of his retarded sister, "The way she listened to the piano was quite unusual. . . . she didn't miss a note. However fast Lipatti played, she caught every single sound that came from the piano. You even felt she was splitting up the harmonies and catching the individual notes. She once told me how many notes there were in this E-flat waltz." The other asks, "Was she able to count so high, then?" The answer is "No. You see, she had a big sheet of paper covered all over with pencil dots, like tiny specks of dust. It was like a photograph of the Milky Way, only with all the heavenly bodies shown as black dots. The opus 18 waltz was all there." "Hikari's role in this novel is very small, and very dark," Kenzaburo now says, but while this is true in a narrow, literal way, there is something that verges on the uncanny in the way Hikari went on to enact—and dramatically surpass—something his father imagined there, something that would have seemed impossible for a child with severe developmental disabilities.

This novel also shows its characters enacting—sometimes very consciously, sometimes quite unknowingly—myths and legends that existed before their lifetimes and replicating their ancestors' lives, and Kenzaburo Oe went on, in many of his later works, to show Hikari-like characters playing mythic roles. And there is something decidedly disconcerting in the way Hikari did in fact go on to live out a story we all know from folk and fairy tales, as though his father could in some way have helped to bring about his extraordinary development just by imagining that something similar could take place. His avowed motive for giving his son a name that means "light" appears to have motivated other choices, too, choices that turned out to be as unforeseeably appropriate as Hikari's prophetic name.

But in 1963, even as his literary imagination was developing constructive possibilities, he was showing a similarly constructive imagination in real life. He and Yukari refused to give up on their seemingly hopeless baby. Their efforts would pay off for reasons they had no way of understanding at the time—reasons that scientists came to understand during later decades, when knowledge about the human brain began growing at an explosive rate, bringing answers to some of the scientific puzzles Hikari presents.

"The Male Celatius"

At the time of the operation, there seemed to be no hope that Hikari would ever achieve anything. The growth on his head had been removed, but he looked deformed, with a conspicuous plastic plate embedded in the back of his skull. He was mostly silent, obviously needier than the average infant but unable to communicate his needs as a normal baby would. Having no tear ducts, he could not even cry.

It is extremely unusual in Japan for fathers to get at all involved in caring for their infants, but both Hikari's parents resolved from the start to exert themselves to the utmost for their problematic baby. "When we brought him home from the hospital," his mother remembers, "it was like trying to take care of some exotic small animal. His condition was so delicate, and we were so afraid for him. We were afraid everything would hurt him, and we didn't know how to protect him." And Kenzaburo was no less determined than Yukari to cherish their vulnerable baby—a determination that would deepen and intensify throughout Hikari's childhood, ultimately evolving into the extraordinary relationship that inspired some of his most moving writing.

Hikari's body had been trained to follow the hospital feeding schedule: every night, he would wake up every three hours. (Frequent awakening is also a classical symptom of autism.) At first he needed only milk, but when he got to be larger, he had to be given juices and strained foods. It was much harder work in those days in Japan taking care even of a normal baby than it later became. Yukari explained, "You could buy formula, but there was no ready-made baby food, and no fruit juice. We had something called 'juice,' but there was very little fruit juice in it. So we had to prepare everything ourselves, from scratch—mashing, pulverizing, straining everything through cloths." And in Hikari's case, because of the particular dangers infections would present to his brain, and from fear that his early life in the completely sanitary environment of the pediatric intensive-care ward had prevented him from developing the usual immunities, all the utensils used to prepare and serve his food and drink had to be thoroughly sterilized after every use. The labor was time-consuming and exhausting, too much even for two young parents working together. Yukari's mother helped a lot.

Hikari was a sickly baby, weak, prone to allergies, catching colds frequently. Yukari spent the first four years of Hikari's life attending to his needs full-time. In Japan in those days, it was as rare

for husbands to help with housework as with babies, but Kenzaburo willingly pitched in with that, too, his chief contribution
being cooking. He knew, of course, that his wife's strength was
taxed to the limit during Hikari's infancy, but although he was
aware of the prevailing prejudice against the disabled, it took him
more than thirty years to discover that when she took their child
out, she suffered from the scorn of her neighbors, as well.

Kenzaburo remembers, "We were not rich in those years. We
were renting an apartment on the second floor of our landlady's
house. We had no bath, no shower"—a private bathroom was still
a luxury in Japan at that time—"so we had to use the public bath-
house. And when she took Hikari there, the women from the
neighborhood would criticize her for taking a disabled child out in
public." This may seem startlingly heartless, but at this time
scarred survivors of the bombings of Hiroshima and Nagasaki were
bathing in rivers because they were forbidden by law to enter public baths. "They believed in segregating the handicapped completely. Some would even mock Hikari, too. But my wife gave me
no idea of this at the time. She never complained—she is a very
strong person. It was only a few months ago, when she talked to a
reporter from a Japanese women's magazine, that I found out what
she had suffered then."

And Kenzaburo remains bitter about the condemnation he
himself suffered then, and has continued to suffer, simply because
he has never hesitated to be seen in public with his handicapped
son: "Japanese society is not as bad now in terms of segregating
handicapped people, but thirty years ago, this was very strong.
When we walked out in the street with Hikari, people laughed and
pointed. I read an essay about some Japanese Christians who lived
in a small village around eighty years ago. One of them had a
handicapped son, and he took the child everywhere with him. At
that time, handicapped children were considered shameful, a se-
cret to be hidden away, so his attitude was very eccentric. The villagers called the father and son a 'chindonya.'" (A *chindonya* is a

noisy promotional band; these days it usually has three players, one beating a drum, one playing a saxophone, one plucking a samisen, who march around a locality in colorful Kabuki makeup and flamboyant theatrical costumes making as much noise as possible to advertise, say, the arrival of a traveling troupe of entertainers or the opening of a new store.) "Even in the postwar period, Hikari and I may have been perceived as a chindonya. I'm considered very strange because I love my boy and I'm proud of him and I always went walking with him.

"In the late 1960s, it became very fashionable in Japan to write about the future. One man wrote that we could look forward in the near future to a world where the handicapped would no longer exist. Progress would somehow cause them to disappear, and they would be abolished in the most natural way. How convenient!"

The Oes' daughter, Natsumiko, may have suffered the most from the unusual attention her parents lavished on her brother. Comparing Hikari's infancy with her daughter's, Yukari gamely said Natsumiko was much easier to take care of, "but nowhere near as interesting." A jolly, active toddler, loving and protective of her big brother from the moment she understood he sometimes needed her help, she became introspective and gloomy after going to a public primary school where classmates tormented her as the child of a lefty writer and the sister of a retarded cripple, as if these two taunts were aspects of a single thing—as, in a way, they were. She did not really cheer up again until she was sent to a private school, where her classmates were the children of well-educated parents, too well-brought-up to say such things. And Natsumiko's early troubles found their way into Kenzaburo's writing, too, if not to the extent of her brother's.

Kenzaburo has often said, and written, that his own experiences with Hikari at this time were instrumental in developing his imagination as a writer. Kenzaburo and Yukari had to use their imaginations constantly in anticipating their son's needs, since he was unable to express them himself. "He did begin to say words when he was four or five," Yukari remembers. "In fact, he was very good at mimicking sounds, and he learned the words to all the lullabies I sang him very quickly. But he gave no sign of understanding the meaning of the sounds he could make. He seemed to know the names of things, but only nouns. He couldn't speak in sentences. He couldn't really use words to express anything, not even very simple things like 'Give me that,' or 'I'm hungry,' or 'It hurts,'" she says. And it was difficult to interpret even his nonverbal ways of expressing himself.

In some ways, Hikari's very problems made him easy to care for, though. He didn't require stimulation or amusement. His favorite plaything was a simple daruma doll—a gourd-shaped, stylized representation of the sixth-century monk Bodhidharma, the founder of Zen Buddhism. He journeyed from India to China, where he is said to have spent nine years in continuous, cross-legged meditation. When he finally got up, his legs fell off; hence the shape of the doll. Because a weight in the toy's hemispherical bottom insures that it will right itself when it is pushed over, these dolls are considered lucky, symbolizing recovery from reversals. They are googly-eyed, with bushy black eyebrows. Often, they are sold with no eyeballs painted in: their owner can make a wish while painting in one of them, then paint in the other when the wish comes true. Hikari's had eyeballs, and his parents thought his attachment to it might have been based on its eyes, because the first person who had cared for him was a nurse in the pediatric ward with huge, round eyes. For whatever reason, he liked having it near him, and he could amuse himself with it for hours on end, contentedly pushing it over again and again. But his parents were not content; how could they resign themselves to watching their son grow up with his activities restricted, as many autistic patients' are, to a series of repetitive motions?

In many ways, his behavior was typical of the autistic. "Most children of that age," his mother says, "are always getting into everything and making a mess, but Hikari wasn't like that at all. He just sat quietly most of the time, and he was very orderly." Ironically, his very orderliness caused problems. "He always needed to arrange things in patterns, and to put things together that seemed as if they should go together. For example, if someone had taken dead flowers out of a vase to throw them away, even if they were actually already in the garbage, he would find a vase or anything you could use for a vase, like a bottle, and put the flowers in it." Yukari took him on regular visits to her mother, who lived in western Japan at that time, undaunted by the long train trips there and back to Tokyo. "One time, at my mother's house, he did something really embarrassing—it was when we were trying to toilet-train him, and he had a little potty with a lid. Well, he was putting the lids on all the pots and pans in her kitchen—this was his need to match things up—and there was one pan that didn't have a lid. He apparently noticed that his potty lid was exactly the right size for it, so he took it off the potty and put it on her cooking pan."

But as he grew, he also showed occasional signs of disorderliness—worrying flashes of willful, independent behavior, in fact. And Kenzaburo, who by this time found his very identity predicated on his son's dependence on him, has written movingly of his ambivalent reactions to Hikari's intermittent attempts to escape it. In an essay in *A Healing Family,* for example, Kenzaburo has written of Hikari's getting lost briefly in a department store when he was five or six. Irritated by Hikari's habit of charging off without warning in his own direction, Kenzaburo simply let him wander off for a minute, then went to look for him, couldn't find him, and panicked, reporting his disappearance so that an announcement was broadcast over the loudspeaker system. After a couple of hours of searching, he spotted his son trudging doggedly up a staircase. Hikari showed no emotion at all, only clutching his father's hand tightly throughout the journey home. Kenzaburo says that he has often thought since then that his family life would have ended completely if anything had happened to Hikari through his negligence. With typically unsentimental kindness, he writes that this memory prompts him to compassion when he reads stories in the newspaper about young mothers who drop their babies on the floor, maddened by their crying: "I have no doubt that there are instinctive emotions that allow us to raise our children lovingly and well; but there is also instinct involved in that sudden, inexplicable anger one can feel toward a baby crying in the night."

But while Hikari's outbreaks of difficult behavior frightened and angered Kenzaburo, the prospect of the rest of his son's life being spent simply enduring in mute, vegetative passivity was equally distressing. When Hikari was a toddler, the Oes believed that he would never learn to speak. His vocal apparatus was not impaired, but he had been diagnosed as autistic and showed no sign of inclination or ability to use words to communicate. His parents noticed that when birdsong could be heard through an open door or window, he would turn his head toward the sound, though. Did it make him smile? They liked to think so, but it was difficult to tell. Kenzaburo bought a series of records of birdcalls, which he and his wife played over and over for their child, encouraging him to respond to the sounds that seemed to interest him. But all their efforts seemed to be for nothing.

In his own way, Kenzaburo could identify with his son's muteness. When he first came to Tokyo as a student, he had been so ashamed of his Shikoku hick's accent that he developed a stutter and tried to speak as little as possible. In a mobile society like the United States, this would have been an adolescent's extreme reaction. In Tokyo, where people with provincial accents can suffer from extreme discrimination, it was prudent.

Facing his son's silence with characteristic constructiveness, Kenzaburo began writing about similarly handicapped boys, and about fathers who find it urgent—even if seemingly hopeless—to find ways to communicate with them. In a 1968 story, "Father, Where Are You Going?," the father of a mute and physically disabled child teaches the boy to run down a hill by running down the hill repeatedly himself and calling his son's name until the child imitates the action. And in the stunning 1969 novella *Teach Us to Outgrow Our Madness*, the protagonist, who is never named but called simply "the fat man," has an "idiot son," also pudgy, whose name is Mori but who is nicknamed Eeyore, which, as pronounced in Japanese, can mean "It's good." (Hikari's nickname had by this time become "Pooh.")

Like Hikari, Mori was born with a "grave defect." A doctor tells his father, "Even if we operate I'm afraid the infant will either die or be an idiot, one or the other." By the time the child is a toddler, the fat man has managed to teach his son to repeat what he hears. The father takes the child out regularly for snacks of pork noodles and Pepsi, for example, and asks him each time, "Eeyore, the pork noodles and the Pepsi-Cola were good?" taking a kind of satisfaction in hearing his son reply, "Eeyore, the pork noodles and the Pepsi-Cola were good!" although it is not at all clear that Eeyore understands the meaning of the sounds he has been taught to reproduce. His father identifies with him, experiences his son's pain physically, and believes he is the only one who can interpret or explain him to others, or somehow mediate between the world and the child.

No bare summary can begin to suggest the intensity of this novella or of the relationship it describes. For all its blackly comic moments, it's a harrowing story in many ways; its description of the "idiot son" going wild with pain and terror at an eye examination is unforgettable. But its description of the relationship of father and son is even more indelible, especially in the pathos of the father's dawning suspicion that he has been deceiving himself in his belief that the child needs him uniquely when it is in fact he who needs the child.

He uses a striking—even startling—image to represent their complicated interdependence, that of an adult male fish who spends his life embedded in the side of his mate. "Until his son began to peel from his consciousness like a scab, the fat man was convinced that he experienced directly whatever physical pain his son was feeling. When he read somewhere that the male celatius, a deep-sea fish common to Danish waters, lived its life attached like a wart to the larger body of the female, he dreamed that he was the female fish suspended deep in the sea with his son embedded in his body like the smaller male, a dream so sweet that waking up was cruel." In this and other passages in *Teach Us to Outgrow Our Madness,* there is something almost erotic in the intensity of the writing about the interdependent consciousness of father and son.

This interdependence had been growing from the moment Hikari was brought home from the hospital as an infant, deepening throughout the child's toddler years. By the time Hikari reached school age, it had become so intense as to seem nearly pathological—not only to a largely unsympathetic society but even, at times, to Kenzaburo himself. Kenzaburo has written often about this interdependence, sometimes dramatizing it movingly, sometimes analyzing it critically, sometimes just fretting over it. Most of the time, Hikari can't express his feelings clearly, and Kenzaburo needs to believe he understands them. But his writings show that he is aware that this is only his own emotional need, and that his guesses about Hikari's inner life may be entirely incorrect, and that when they are, they may be somehow harmful to Hikari.

Like the handicapped children in Kenzaburo's stories from this period, Hikari was singularly unresponsive as a toddler. But he continued to seem interested in birdsong. Unable to be sure what, if anything, might give his young son pleasure and willing to try anything that seemed likely at all, Kenzaburo concentrated desperately on the series of records of the songs of birds native to Japan. On these, the bird would make its characteristic sound, then an announcer would identify its species. The Oes played the records over and over. It was still difficult to tell whether the sounds interested Hikari.

Then, in 1969, when Hikari was six years old, a breakthrough rewarded Kenzaburo and Yukari. Kenzaburo took Hikari for a walk in the woods one summer day in North Karuizawa, where the family was vacationing. A bird's cry broke the stillness. Kenzaburo heard a voice say, "It's a water rail." The voice sounded like the voice of the announcer on the bird-call records, speaking with the same precise intonation. The writer thought his mind was playing tricks on him, that the water rail's cry had triggered a particularly vivid recollection of the announcement that always followed it. But then the bird sang again, and Kenzaburo heard the voice say, again, "It's a water rail." For the first time in his life, Hikari seemed to be truly speaking—that is, using words to communicate, rather than simply reproducing sounds. Or was it just that the sound the bird made had provided a cue for Hikari to imitate the series of sounds that usually followed it on the record?

Of course, Kenzaburo, for all the singularity of his involvement in coaxing Hikari to communicate, was not striving alone. Yukari had been equally involved with their son's communication difficulties, listening hopefully to all his early utterances for signs of some understanding behind them. "The story about the bird singing has become famous as the first time Hikari spoke," Yukari says. "But we can't be sure it really was. After all, he *was* uttering words before that. But it was the first time we could see any clear meaning behind the words, and the first time we could think he understood the meaning."

After that, Kenzaburo and Yukari continued to play the records over and over for Hikari. But now they began encouraging him to speak by playing only the birdcall, then lifting the needle before the announcer's voice identified the bird. Hikari would supply the identification, always correctly. He had accurately memorized all the melodies; there were more than seventy.

His parents' efforts, continued despite doctors' insistence that they were wasting their time, were paying off now: Hikari began, after a fashion, to speak. Often, his speech took the form of simply repeating what someone had just said to him. At other times, the connection between his reply and the thing he was replying to was mysterious. And there were many times when he did not speak at all, as if he had forgotten that he could do such a thing. Although press accounts of Hikari's development have always been narratives where the hitherto mute child suddenly identified a bird one day and, from that time forth, began to speak, the reality is less dramatic; the moment when it became indubitable that Hikari could speak is not clear-cut. Hikari's brother, Sakurao, was born at about the time Hikari identified the water rail. Yukari can't remember which happened first, Hikari's beginning to speak or the birth of her second son: "Hikari's speaking was a gradual thing."

In addition to the communication problems of autism, Hikari was plagued with physical problems typical for children born with encephalocele. Though he was always a big, strong boy and physically healthy, his coordination did not develop normally, and he could not play like a normal child. His abnormalities dominated Kenzaburo's and Yukari's thoughts, but his parents did their best to protect their other children. Sakurao was scarcely aware of his brother's condition. "When I think back on it now," Sakurao wrote, "it's strange to realize that my older brother and I rarely played together like male siblings in other families. At the time, I never thought of that as odd. He may have enjoyed playing with my sister more, but it may also have been because I enjoyed playing by myself."*

Natsumiko, closer in age to Hikari, had taken it upon herself to be his protector from an early age. His father was his chief mediator with the world, but his sister often played that role within the family. Yukari says, "Trying to raise my three children together when they were all small was really very difficult, and Natsumiko was an enormous help. When she was still quite young, we told her that if we were to die she would have to take care of Hikari, and she took it very seriously. When the children got into fights, we told them they had to be good to each other and not be selfish, and Natsumiko was the one who really took that to heart."

*Translation by Anita Keire.

Singularly vulnerable, Hikari needed all the protectors he could get, both at home and in the outside world. His father's image of the male celatius, sheltered forever by his mate's large body, is a poignant expression of the anxieties Hikari caused on the occasions when he did become detached from his family. "He got lost a few times, as a child," Yukari remembers, "because he had a way of just going off abruptly and then, because his vision is so bad, he wouldn't be able to see us even if we were only a few feet away, so he wouldn't know where to head to join up with us again. Usually, we could find him at once because we could still see him, but once he disappeared in Ikebukuro"—a crowded shopping and entertainment district of Tokyo—"and we were absolutely terrified." Any parents would be distraught about any child's being lost in such a place, of course, but Hikari's difficulties with communication made the situation far worse than it would be with a normal child, and in this case he was found speedily only because the first adult who spoke to him happened, by pure chance, to use a form of words he would respond to: "But when we went to the nearest police box to report his disappearance, he was right there, just because the person who found him, instead of asking, 'What's the matter?'—which was a question he never answered—had happened to ask, 'Are you lost?'"

He sometimes got lost even when his parents were nearby, since he could not see them from even a very short distance. His vision was, and is, extremely poor: on a scale where normal vision is expressed as 1, his is .03. As a toddler, before he got eyeglasses, he could barely see at all. The structure of his brain made it impossible for him to integrate the images from his eyes, which meant that he was unable to judge depth with any accuracy. To get an idea of how far away something was, he had to close one eye. He watched television with his face almost up against the screen.

His eyeglasses mitigated but did not solve these problems. Recently, Hikari was taken to a circus. His seat was quite high up, and he talked afterwards of having seen crocodiles when there had in fact been no crocodiles there. Apparently, his perspective was so foreshortened that he saw animals like lions and tigers as nearly legless, crawling around on the ground.

His vision problems have always made it particularly difficult for him to control his movements precisely, too. But they undoubtedly enabled—and possibly even forced—him to develop a more acute sensitivity to sound. Kenzaburo has written that "since faces and expressions—what people 'look' like—are so difficult for him to make out, he seems to have developed the habit of using his keen hearing to discern a person's character from the 'look' of their voice."

Disabilities can sometimes engender special abilities in such ways. When he was eight years old, Hikari was enrolled in a special-education class in Tokyo. He had always responded more strongly to melody than to any other kind of stimulus, and this continued to be true even after he was exposed, in school, to a wide new range of experiences.

It was at that time that his mother began to realize he had special musical abilities. He would correctly identify the keys of songs he knew when they were played on records or the radio. His mother noticed, too, that while he might be slow to absorb any other kind of information, he always remembered the title of any piece of music, even if he had heard it only once.

Kenzaburo wrote a novel, *The Waters Are Come in Unto My Soul,* published when Hikari was ten, that provides dramatic evidence of the strength of the bond between father and son at that time. Kenzaburo, along with many critics, considers it one of his most important works. It depicts a fantastic apocalypse, with a retarded boy named Jin emerging as the only hope for the future of the human race. His father, calling himself Oki (Big Tree) Isana (Whale), turns his back on the world to retire to a nuclear-fallout shelter with the child.

Beside being retarded and of supreme importance to his father, Jin is like Hikari in several other ways. He is described as having listened every day, at the age of five, to tapes his father made of birdsong and whale noises, accurately identifying them. His father, like Mori's father in *Teach Us to Outgrow Our Madness,* actually experiences the physical pain his child feels. And in another echo of the earlier work and of Hikari's early life, the dialogue of father and son consists of the son's repeating what the father has just said.

Two years after this novel was published, just when Hikari's talent was first beginning to be identified, Hikari had a horrible experience that was as traumatic for his family as for him. Before this, his parents had thought Hikari's wandering off, getting separated from them and lost, was the worst that could possibly happen—and whenever it did, they had been forced to confront their most harrowing fears about him. They couldn't imagine anything worse than these accidental separations from their peculiarly vulnerable and dependent child. But there *was* something worse, and now they found out what it was. Hikari was kidnapped. He was twelve years old.

Kenzaburo, as a controversial writer in a period of political turbulence in Japan, has exposed his family to considerable harassment. In addition, his unconventional pride in his handicapped son has attracted attacks, and his activities in support of the full integration of the handicapped in Japanese society is one of the liberal stances that have provoked the wrath of conservatives against him. And as his celebrity stature grew, he was increasingly a target for kooks of all kinds, who often extended their attentions to the people close to him. Since the stone throwing and harrassing and threatening phone calls that began shortly after his marriage, Kenzaburo's consistent moral courage has continued to subject his family to attacks of various kinds, private and public, and it is plain from his writings that he is tormented by feeling responsible for what his family has suffered from the enemies his writings and political activities have made.

Kenzaburo says that when he recounted Hikari's kidnapping in *Rise Up, O Young Men of the New Age,* the half-factual, half-fictional book of memories and reflections that he wrote about Hikari in 1983, he gave an entirely accurate account, with only the ideologies of the kidnappers fictionalized. The real motives for their actions can never be known. The men were never caught, and their act was so insane that it is doubtful that interrogation would have brought a coherent rationale to light in any case. They did provide hints that ideology had something to do with it, though, and in adumbrating these hints, Kenzaburo had many experiences of ideologically motivated attacks to draw on.

Two young men came to visit him one day, claiming to be students who hoped to study his thesis on Jean-Paul Sartre. They said they had come at the suggestion of the professor who had been Kenzaburo's mentor when he himself was a student.

They were amiable at first, but when the conversation turned to the student movement and its ideology, they became rude, criticizing Oe's ideas scornfully and calling one of his essays "laughable." At the same time, one of them seemed disconcertingly familiar with Oe's habits. Yukari had left the men together; worried by the tones of their voices, she returned to the room with Hikari in tow. Abruptly, the so-called students became polite, and took their leave.

Soon after that, Kenzaburo went to escort Hikari home from school one snowy day. He waited and waited, but Hikari never came. Kenzaburo and Yukari searched the neighborhood frantically in alternation, with one staying home to care for the younger children while the other looked for Hikari. When Kenzaburo was home, whenever he heard the telephone ring, he thought it would be a neurotic student who had harassed him with telephone calls and letters for years, and who, he thought, would be the likeliest person to kidnap or harm Hikari, because he was obsessed with the boy, having repeatedly told Kenzaburo that he was a hypocrite since he helped no one in society but his own idiot son.

But it turned out to have nothing to do with the man who had been harassing him in those terms. Finally, in the evening, a phone call came from one of the young men. He said that the other had taken Hikari because he was irritated by Kenzaburo's being anti-establishment without any concrete political commitment; he thought that by taking Hikari he could force Kenzaburo to confront the real world. But the kidnapper had given up his original plan and instead simply abandoned the boy at Tokyo Station.

Tokyo Station must be a terrifying place for a mentally disabled child. It's enormous, full of hordes of people rushing to and fro as though stampeding. Grand Central Station seems uncrowded and tranquil in comparison.

After three hours of searching through the huge, labyrinthine station, Kenzaburo spotted his son on a platform, just standing still, watching the snow on the rails. His pants were soaked, and the rain boots he was wearing were filled with his own urine. As he looked up at his father, his face showed no emotion, but the tension in his small body was obvious. After a while, Kenzaburo could feel him beginning to relax. Kenzaburo himself was so upset that he vomited and was so angry that he could not help shouting. Once they got home, Yukari began worrying about what might happen if Kenzaburo ever found the kidnapper; his anger was, understandably enough, so extreme.

Kenzaburo says that he and his wife had not informed the police or the press, being afraid that any publicity the crime received might set off more attacks. "The police knew about it, though, because I talked to people at Tokyo Station, and they told the police." At the time, the school Hikari was attending was so close to the Oes' house that they sometimes let him walk to and from school unescorted, though some family member often waited for him outside. And Kenzaburo says he felt particularly vulnerable because at that time, his publisher had issued a directory of authors that included his name and address, which is customary for Japanese publishers. So anyone reading an account of how Hikari was kidnapped would easily be able to duplicate the crime. "These two young men had told him they were taking him to a concert or something, and so he went off with them."

There is an odd postscript to Hikari's kidnapping in *Rise Up*. Ten years later, newspapers reported that two former student activists with the same names as the kidnappers had been beaten to death. Three days after that, one of the actual kidnappers called the Oes' house to explain that he and his accomplice had only been using the activists' names then. He said he was just calling to let the family know that he and his accomplice were actually still alive.

When Yukari railed at him, saying that little Hikari might have died, he responded by saying it might have been better if he *had* died, freeing Yukari from the burden of caring for him and forcing Kenzaburo to confront reality. He added that, in any case, a child with a mental disability could never be productive. Then he said he would call back at ten that night, when Kenzaburo would be home.

When Kenzaburo returned, Yukari told him all about the telephone call, and all three of their children heard what she said. Just before ten, Hikari, who was supposed to be in bed, came downstairs to the living room. Kenzaburo assumed that he had forgotten to take the antiseizure medication he was supposed to take every night and was coming to get it now, but in fact he had come to intercept the expected phone call. When the phone rang, he grabbed the receiver, and when Kenzaburo tried to take it from him, Hikari pushed him away as hard as he could.

"You are a bad person!" he said into the receiver. "I do not know why you are laughing! I cannot talk to you! Nothing! At all!"† and slammed the receiver down.

He was very upset, and his mother asked him whether he still remembered what had been done to him nearly ten years before. And was he still angry about it? She told her husband she was afraid that their son's rage might cause a seizure, or that he might become violent.

---

†The dagger here, and throughout the chapter, follows translations by Yoshiko Kuwahara.

Hikari said, "I have never forgotten! That was a bad person! But, Mom, don't worry! I won't be angry again! Because there are no bad people anymore!"† In fact, the Oes had no way of knowing whether the kidnappers were on the other end of the line. They have questioned Hikari repeatedly, but he has always refused to tell them whom he was speaking to, so they can only guess. "We still don't know," Kenzaburo says.

Kenzaburo has been so haunted by the memory of Hikari's disappearance that he has nightmares even today about accidents in which Hikari is lost forever. "I think I'm always writing about this incident, in different ways," he says. The most direct expression of the way he felt about it is undoubtedly in a novel, *The Pinch Runner Memorandum,* published one year after the crime, in 1976, when Hikari was thirteen. It contains a scene obviously inspired by his memories of the incident, and he says the book "contains my real emotions about the kidnapping."

It is a very complicated and highly fantastical novel: the story is presented as being told by Kenzaburo Oe, the novelist father of a brain-damaged son called Hikari, as a "ghostwriter" for another father of a brain-damaged child, whose condition is just like Hikari's. This child is called Mori, like the child in *Teach Us to Outgrow Our Madness.* Just like Hikari, this child has a plastic plate in his skull covering the hole left after surgery for encephalocele. The two fathers meet while waiting to pick up their sons from school. The identification of the father with the child is taken further here than in the earlier works: Mori's father and Mori are "switched over"—they actually turn into each other; the eight-year-old son becomes twenty-eight and the thirty-year-old father becomes eighteen, and the two exchange consciousness, in a way.

In this novel, Mori is not kidnapped but simply gets lost at Tokyo Station. His condition, of course, makes his disappearance particularly worrisome and adds to the difficulty of finding him. "Mori's eight years old, all right, but he won't tell you his name if you ask him. Besides, he won't show any of the anxiety that might tip someone off that he's a missing child," his father thinks. "The structure of the building itself is rather simple, but Tokyo Station has a tremendous depth to it, a perfect labyrinth for children like *our children;* besides, you know that down there tracks shoot off to every part of Japan." And later, "I couldn't shake off an obsessive image of Mori dumped at Tokyo Station like an abandoned orphan in a coin-op locker." (This was, and still is, a common way of getting rid of unwanted babies in Japan.) "I was also bedeviled by the possibility that Mori had chosen a train at random, taken off to a faraway place, and would be brought up by a stranger. Even if lost for only a few weeks, he'd lose *ties* of friendship with his own father and be completely transformed; by the time I found him, he might have turned into one of those children with the vacant stare of a stray dog, with a strange scar on the lower part of his abdomen. . . . When I thought about the possibility of him falling from the platform, of being run over by a train, I felt my entire inner self gutted. The child, abandoned, missing, not quite understanding what had happened to him, lingering alone in a strange place." And the father's anger leads to a farcical and unrealistic but disturbing scene in which he beats his disabled son and is, in turn, attacked with a razor by his wife.

Kenzaburo's bond with Hikari had grown to the point that he could not only imagine an interchange of their identities but felt Hikari's existence to be so crucial that he could extend its importance far enough beyond himself to include—everything. In *The Pinch Runner Memorandum,* even contemplating the possibility of losing his son led him to extend scenes of chaotic total personal breakdown to nothing less than the threat of nuclear destruction of the world. And Hikari's dependence on both Kenzaburo and Yukari was, of course, still nearly absolute. Yet at the same time, the boy had begun showing signs of the talent that would lead him to independent achievement—and to being heard by the world directly instead of through the medium of his father's literary imagination.

Becoming a Composer

Hikari has been hearing music all his life. During her pregnancy, his mother listened to lots of Mozart. "They say fetuses begin to hear during their fifth month in the womb," she says, "so maybe he started to like it then." And after he was born, to alleviate her depression, she played recordings of the works of her other favorite classical composers—Chopin and Beethoven, chiefly—over and over. "When he was a toddler, he loved Western classical music. He would listen to it for hours, perfectly absorbed. Whenever we wanted some peace, we'd just put a few symphonies on the record player, and we could be sure Pooh-chan wouldn't bother us at all. At that time, I had no idea how unusual that was. It wasn't until I had my other children that I realized that most normal toddlers won't listen to *any* kind of music for hours in a row—and that Western classical music is something most of them get tired of very fast."

Not Hikari. In a memoir about him, she wrote of how, when he was an infant, she played her favorite Western classical composers again and again until the records wore out. When a worn-out record stuck and repeated a passage, Hikari wailed, as he did when a record stopped. She could quiet him only by playing another record. At first, she thought he enjoyed only Western classical music, but by the time he was a toddler she discovered that he liked children's songs and some other music, too. She also discovered that he could remember any tune he had ever heard. Entering a restaurant with his family, if classical music was being played, he could tell them at once what the piece was, even after hearing only a few notes.

When he was nine, Yukari began teaching him to read music and to play the piano, reasoning that even if he never got to be very good at it, the attempt might improve his coordination, and even if it didn't, he would probably enjoy it. Every day when he came home from school, all he wanted to do was listen to classical music. Many autistic people limit their activities very narrowly; a tendency to have interests that are both highly restricted and very intense is listed in the diagnostic manual of the American Psychiatric Association as a symptom of autism. It can also be characteristic of genius, of course, but at this time no one suspected that Hikari's preoccupation would ultimately lead him to transcend the usual limits of his condition.

Hikari's physical handicaps precluded his developing much

skill as a pianist. It was hard for him to see the notes and to see and control his fingers on the keys. But he clearly had interest in and aptitude for music. He mastered the contents of Japan's standard introductory piano textbook very quickly. He enjoyed the lessons with his mother, and he had perfect pitch—the ability to correctly identify any note heard instantly and to sing any tone accurately.

Inborn absolute pitch is rare. Musicians can be trained to develop relative pitch—that is, the ability to identify notes through recognizing intervals from given memorized pitches—and the earlier they begin musical training, the more likely they are to develop it. There is no definitive figure for the occurrence of inborn perfect pitch in the general population, since the phenomenon has chiefly been studied in musicians, but it is usually estimated as less than 4 percent. It is more common in people with disabilities like Hikari's, and it has recently been linked to a particular gene.

Hikari was extraordinarily sensitive to sounds of all kinds. He had (and to some extent still has) a horror of dogs, apparently because he disliked their barking and growling so. He had an excellent memory for the sounds of spoken language, too. He enjoyed exploiting the comic possibilities of language and was always making puns. And he was—and still is—a talented mimic; he could reproduce the routines of popular television entertainers. And he could remember nearly any piece of music he heard, even music he didn't like particularly. He could even remember the atonal music he detested, if the piece wasn't too long or complicated. What he remembered best, though, was the eighteenth- and nineteenth-century Western classical music he preferred.

Although such talents made him easy to teach in some ways, Yukari, having three children to take care of, would probably not have been able to instruct him at all if Natsumiko had not proven extraordinarily helpful in taking care of Hikari. Even as a toddler, she understood that her brother needed her help and assumed responsibilities far beyond what might be expected at her age. When her mother went shopping with the children, Natsumiko would take care of the other two. By the time she was six—an age when most children need a parent to escort them when using a public bathroom—she was able to escort Hikari, who couldn't manage such things by himself. (In Japan at that time, most public toilets were unisex.) At home, she often took over the care of her brothers, freeing her mother to get on with her chores. Still, Yukari couldn't manage to give Hikari piano lessons—or even help with practicing—every day, and in any case she had only a beginner's skills herself, having taken lessons for a few years as a child.

Trouble began when Hikari, at age eleven, reached the point of trying to play with both hands simultaneously. He simply couldn't do it, and he stopped making progress. She reprimanded him for not trying hard enough; after all, he had been able to learn everything up to that time, however slowly and laboriously. As his parent, she wanted him to do well and became disappointed and frustrated when he couldn't. And he, of course, wanted to please her and earn her approval, so he, too, became disappointed and frustrated. The lessons weren't fun anymore; in fact, they had become something to be dreaded. Yukari thought it would be a terrible shame if he should come to hate playing the piano, when he seemed to love music more than anything else in the world.

A more knowledgeable teacher was the only solution. The Oes asked around among friends and acquaintances, trying to find someone willing and able to work with a pupil with special needs. Finally, Kumiko Tamura, an amateur classical singer, member of a chorus group, and the wife of a friend of Kenzaburo's, agreed to try, coming to the Oes' house for an hour once every two weeks.

She hadn't been informed in advance about Hikari's disabilities, and once his mother explained his condition, she concluded that she might best begin by teaching him to sing songs with her. She had never worked with a handicapped child before, but she and Hikari got along well from the start. When she found that he could already play the piano a little, she began teaching him to play chords, because his poor physical coordination ruled out the usual fingering exercises.

At first, communication was difficult, and Yukari had to serve as an interpreter at every lesson. But after a couple of months, as they grew used to each other, Ms. Tamura and Hikari were able to talk to each other without her aid, and the lessons became weekly. After the first year, Hikari and his teacher found a way to communicate fluently about musical concepts that were beyond Yukari's level of knowledge, and she couldn't understand what they were saying to each other at all. Ms. Tamura's willingness to accommodate her problematic pupil undoubtedly accelerated their achievements in communicating: in a memoir she wrote a few years ago, Yukari said, "What Hikari likes about his teacher is that she never forces him to practice. Hikari doesn't like to be told what to do and what not to do. He likes to do everything his own way. His teacher knows that and that's why Hikari gets along very well with her."

Among other things, Ms. Tamura taught him to improvise. Sometimes she would play a melody and he would continue it; sometimes the two of them would work out a harmony together. "At such times it often happened that we would come up with a particularly attractive melody or harmony which it seemed a pity to lose, although . . . often . . . Hikari remembered such interesting passages and repeated them later," Ms. Tamura has written in the liner notes for his first CD. This was why she began teaching him how to write down the tunes he made up. He progressed rapidly; soon he could accurately write down anything she played for him. "I was especially eager for him to learn to transcribe music," Yukari remembers. "I had read about how Mozart would write down music as his father played it, and it seemed like the kind of thing Hikari would enjoy a lot."

It wasn't long before he had transcribed music from nearly every record the Oes owned. He enjoyed using his transcribing skills just for fun. He has always loved his maternal grandmother, who lived with the family off and on over the years, always treating him very affectionately. "Once, when Hikari was still in elementary school, she was hospitalized briefly and we went to visit her. She told him she wanted to find a particular song. She didn't know who wrote it and couldn't remember anything about it but the melody. He took her request very seriously, and wrote the tune down for her on music paper as soon as he got home," Yukari said.

On another occasion, Kenzaburo had been watching a videotape when Hikari was in the room and told him afterward that he had liked the soundtrack, which had been composed by Toru Takemitsu, Japan's best-known composer. His highly original music had made him a celebrity in Japan at an early age, and in 1964, when he was thirty-four, the huge international success of the film *Woman in the Dunes,* with his haunting, otherworldly score, brought him fame all over the world. *November Steps,* a New York Philharmonic commission, a sensation when it was first performed in 1967 and still one of his best-loved pieces, solidified his reputation in the West. Takemitsu, one of Kenzaburo's oldest and closest friends, had been one of the first people he talked to about his son's condition, right after Hikari's birth. And Takemitsu got along in a friendly way with the grown-up Hikari. Kenzaburo especially liked the music for a particular scene in the tape he had been watching, about four minutes long, where a young woman was eating an apple. Hikari promptly transcribed it for him, then played it on the piano as well as he could. Later, Kenzaburo told Takemitsu about it. A journalist who was with them didn't believe that Hikari could have transcribed the music correctly from memory, but Kenzaburo happened to have the notebook Hikari had used and gave it to Takemitsu to check. The composer said it was exactly what he had written, with only a minor error or two.

Hikari had always enjoyed his lessons with Ms. Tamura, but now he could hardly wait for them. When entering a Japanese house, people normally exchange their shoes for slippers at the threshold. Hikari would greet Ms. Tamura at the door carrying not only slippers for her to put on but also an alarm clock set for the time the lesson was to begin; he apparently wanted to make certain that none of the time sacred to music was wasted on pleasantries.

He would show her what he had written in his music-manuscript notebook since the last time they met. At first, these were bits and pieces of music he had heard. But soon, by the time he was thirteen, he began writing down fragments he had composed himself, working entirely in his head, without a piano. At first, Ms. Tamura did not know what they were. His favorite compositional method at that time was filling up a manuscript page with broken chords or Alberti basses (a particular left-hand accompaniment of broken triads popular in the classical period), then thinking up a melody to go with them. He wrote mostly in an eighteenth-century idiom, and she thought he must have heard something on the radio that she did not happen to recognize.

His mother thought so, too. "He was always listening to classical music, and he could remember whatever he heard. He knew many more pieces than I did, so I always assumed that he was writing down things I just didn't happen to know." She said in a television interview that although Hikari would write "This Is My Song" on his music manuscripts, she told Ms. Tamura that he must just be transcribing things he'd heard.

But the day came when his teacher saw four measures she was absolutely certain were his and no one else's. As she put it, in the same television interview, "I yelled out, 'Mrs. Oe, Hikari's composing!' I'm embarrassed to say this, but it reminded me of Annie Sullivan and Helen Keller and the water breakthrough. It was an emotional moment. I couldn't stop crying."

She told a Japanese magazine reporter some details about Hikari's progress: "While having fun with various keys, Hikari began to show very clear likes and dislikes about which keys were good for particular pieces. Hikari remembers everything that he plays on any given day because he has a good memory, and so we started listening practice, too, because he also has a good ear. Listening to the music, he writes it down on a score sheet and afterwards even goes so far as to write in the chords, having thought intently on it for a while. He also does the opposite, writing in the melody while listening to the harmony. He started to write a lot of melodies on notepads the way a small child draws pictures. A lot of these doodled score sheets started to pile up, but after a while I realized that there were pieces that I did not recognize mixed in. They appeared to be Hikari's own compositions. I really could not have been happier at the time! Still, I wondered at first if they might possibly be scores that I didn't know, because he knows everything when it comes to classical music, from symphonic to instrumental pieces."* Gradually, though, Ms. Tamura realized that all the works she couldn't identify were entirely Hikari's. And the day came when this was true of everything he wrote in the notebook.

It is not clear when Hikari himself realized that he was composing. He was thirteen when he presented his teacher with the finished score of a short piece by leaving it on the music rack of the piano encircled with a red ribbon tied in a bow; he seemed to know it was something he had made all by himself. "Birthday Waltz," written for his sister's birthday, was his first finished composition.

And when he graduated from elementary school, he wrote a setting for a poem his father had written called "Graduation." Kenzaburo, as always, took great pride and pleasure in his son's musical development. "Sitting nearby with a book, listening to his piano lessons," he wrote, "I can feel the best, most human things in his character finding lively and fluent expression."

Hikari's siblings were in some awe of his talents. His brother, Sakurao, recalled, "One of the most inspiring things for me from my childhood was when my brother composed music with his piano teacher. Since I had no interest in music as such, it was beyond the bounds of my understanding that my brother remembered countless classical composition names, or that he was doing this thing which I knew nothing about, called "composing." In

*The asterisk here, and throughout the chapter, follows translations by Anita Keire.

light of this, my older brother, the musician, may not have been someone I related to very well as a young child. As far as I'm concerned, my brother in his younger days was both a musician and a big sumo fan. There was no need for me to be conscious of my brother's handicaps when it came to these two points."*

Ms. Tamura remembers that Hikari, who had always been quite timid, began to seem much more self-confident as his skill grew. Soon he was regularly presenting her with short (under three minutes playing time) but fully finished pieces, mostly in his favorite keys, E and B.

Kenzaburo believes that Hikari was happiest from the ages of ten to fifteen. He had begun to discover and enjoy his musical abilities, and his health had not yet begun to hinder the activities he found rewarding. These were his strongest and healthiest years. His father has written of how Hikari would race his brother and sister down the hill on summer mornings at their North Karuizwa cottage; despite his physical problems, he was usually the winner of what the children called their "marathon."

When he was fifteen, he had his first seizure, an event his family found mysterious and frightening. It was not entirely unexpected, though; 25 percent of autistic patients develop seizure disorders during adolescence. The seizures, which doctors have diagnosed as epileptic, have continued, and whenever he has one, Hikari is left exhausted and afraid. The anticonvulsive medications he must take to control them have unfortunate side effects: they are depressants and they irritate his gums, aggravating problems he has always had with his teeth.

Hikari's seizures meant that his family had to take better care of him, never relaxing their vigilance. "I believe it was when I was about ten years old that I began to be conscious of my older brother Hikari's handicap," Sakurao wrote. "Prior to that, I understood that he had entered a special class in elementary school and that he was older than his grade level, etc., but I do not remember wondering about the reason for these things or giving it much thought. The thing that made me conscious of the fact that my older brother is handicapped was when he began to have occasional seizures. When seizures occurred, it worried me that his eyes would become temporarily unable to see, or that my brother was withstanding some sort of pain that I could not know. Of course, I understood at the time that he was known as a 'mentally retarded' person, but I do not recall ever worrying about these things myself. What I was concerned about was not my brother's intellect, but that he would be in grave physical danger if he were to have a seizure when no one was with him."* Sakurao went on to explain, though, that he was as self-centered as any normal child, so his childhood was not really blighted by concern for his brother's health.

Hikari's health wavered through the years, but his composing continued, with only brief interruptions, through all his vicissitudes. Yukari says he creates most of his music while sitting Japanese-style on the carpet at home, with calluses on his ankles testifying to the amount of time he spends that way. He devotes much conscious thought to choosing the keys for his pieces and to their titles. Sometimes he asks family members for help in titling; Yukari, for example, suggested that he call one piece "Magic Flute" and another "Pied Piper." More often, he seeks a consensus on titles he has already chosen. And music has never lost the power to cheer and comfort him. He has such faith in its healing power that whenever family members or guests seem sad or unwell, Hikari insists on putting some music on the stereo for them.

As Hikari came into his late teens, his family quietly encouraged his musical activities. He continued composing and broadened his musical education by devoutly watching all the music-instruction programs on Channel 3, Tokyo's educational station. At that time, many offered instruction in the koto, samisen, guitar, piano, and other popular instruments. He never missed a broadcast and often continued to investigate the characteristics of the instruments to which he had been introduced in this way. In his senior high school years, he wrote for the guitar, flute, and violin as well as for the piano. He tried writing vocal music only once, starting something for four voices; he never finished it.

Kenzaburo began to hope at that time that Hikari would be able to communicate with other retarded people through his music. In the partly fictional, partly factual memoir of Hikari that he wrote when his son came of age, he described an imaginary occasion when he and Hikari were asked to create a musical for a home for disabled children. At its conclusion, the teacher who had extended the original invitation announced to the audience that the composer was there, and asked Hikari to leave the wings and take a bow. But Hikari shyly lingered backstage, thanking the audience from the wings and asking that they join in the singing of the finale, which he conducted without emerging onstage. Kenzaburo wrote poignantly of applauding his son's shadow on that triumphant occasion.

This fantasy was written in a spirit of hope. "At that time," Kenzaburo recalls, "schools for disabled children were very closed worlds. They were all protecting their own students from outsiders, and they would never have invited us to come. The scene was just my dream for my Hikari then. Now, all that has changed, and we are often invited by schools and institutions of that kind."

But some of Hikari's pieces were performed in local concerts in those days, including one he wrote at eighteen, when he graduated from the Seicho Municipal School for the Handicapped, in 1981. While he was still a student there, a "welfare workplace"—an occupational training center for the mentally handicapped—was being constructed nearby, and some local residents protested its construction. On one occasion, Kenzaburo, when he went to pick Hikari up after school, saw three affluent-seeming women from the protesting group standing outside the school gate, looking at the building. One said, disapprovingly, "It's too nice." They had surrounded Hikari, who stood silently, with his head down, until rescued by Kenzaburo and another disabled child's parent.

Kenzaburo learned that Hikari had at first been speaking to them in a friendly way. But no matter how often he was asked, Hikari always refused to tell what they had said. As reported later on television news about the protests, their group was so opposed to having an occupational center for the mentally disabled in their neighborhood that they were prepared to pay ten million yen to stop its construction.

Kenzaburo wrote a novel, *Echo of Heaven,* much later—it was published in 1989—which gives a few glimpses of Hikari at this time of his life. These glimpses don't shed much light on Hikari himself, but the book as a whole can tell us a good deal about the way Kenzaburo's sense of his relationship with his son had evolved by that time. Kenzaburo narrates this novel as a famous novelist named K who is the father of a musical, retarded son named Hikari, who appears in the novel simply as himself, in a rather peripheral role. The main character, Marie, is the mother of a schoolmate of Hikari's at Aodori, his actual school. There is a scene where she attends a performance of Bach's *St. John Passion* with her son; Kenzaburo and Hikari are there, too. "Parents of handicapped children make a point of choosing seats near an exit, knowing that the child may have to go to the bathroom during the performance, that his movements are awkward, that he may do something unexpected."

There is a scene at the private club where Kenzaburo took Hikari swimming in real life, a club that makes many appearances in his writing. Besides her retarded son, Marie has another son who has been crippled in an accident. In the course of the novel, these two children commit suicide together, the crippled one persuading his retarded brother to push his wheelchair off a cliff, then jump off himself.

Hikari has nothing to do with that. His appearances in the story are undramatic and entirely plausible. However, there is a chilling description of his acting up at a medical examination and having a seizure afterward, slipping as he descends from a train with his mother. Miserable and embarrassed, he says, very slowly, "Su-i-cide." Later in the book, Marie tells K, "You're lucky to have Hikari. . . . He's a companion to you, or maybe a medium."

As a character in the novel, he is unimportant, but he is an important presence in the book in another way. It contains many strongly felt statements about retarded children, society's attitudes to them, their education, their parents' relationships with them, and the spiritual consequences to parents both of having children who have been dealt such an unfair hand by fate and of having lives that, because of those children, are necessarily exceptionally difficult.

But there is another, more deeply personal sense in which Hikari is important in this novel. Surveying all the fiction Kenzaburo Oe has written that uses characters who are mentally disabled, a reader is forced to conclude that he has been involved in a rather compulsive exploration, systematic yet perhaps not entirely conscious, of the possibilities Hikari's existence presented at various times. At the beginning, *A Personal Matter,* the first fictional work directly inspired by Hikari's birth, raises the possibility that a baby like Hikari, instead of destroying his parent as society seems to expect, could somehow save him. "Aghwee" shows a parent destroying himself by deciding to let a baby like Hikari die. The institutionalization of one retarded child in *The Silent Cry* has destructive consequences, as does the rural seclusion of another. *Teach Us to Outgrow Our Madness* presents some of the darker aspects of the father and son's mutual dependence and ends with the father's realization that his son can get along without him "as an idiot, in an idiot's way." *The Waters Are Come in Unto My Soul* may show Kenzaburo's awareness of the way his absorption in his son has enabled him to escape from society, but like *The Pinch Runner Memorandum,* it's also a statement about the constructive possibilities of such an escape that he has realized in literary creation.

By the time Kenzaburo wrote *An Echo of Heaven,* he was ready to imagine what the loss of a child in such an intensely mutually

dependent relationship might entail. In part, the book is a harrowing account of a character who loses her two handicapped children.
Such a loss would be conventionally viewed as a deliverance, but in
this novel the loss destroys the bereaved mother. Seeking to find a
means of continuing her life without the retarded son who had
given her a sense of purpose, she becomes involved with an eccentric Japanese cult in Mexico, where she dies. In fact, her activities
may have had some constructive results—her story is complicated
and ambiguous—but the loss of her child unquestionably precluded any kind of conventional human fulfillment for her.

In real life, after his graduation, Hikari began attending a center similar to the one that the women in his neighborhood had
been trying to block: the Karasuyama Occupational Therapy Center, in western Tokyo. He went there five days a week. He could
not take public transportation by himself and, of course, did not
drive, so he was escorted to and from the center by a family member. It is an hour and a half from the Oes' home, and the commute
involves taking both a bus and a train.

He still goes there today. Various members of the family have
had the responsibility of escorting him at different times. It is a
heavy responsibility. On the way from the station to the center,
Hikari must negotiate two hazardous crosswalks very carefully;
having a seizure there in the midst of onrushing traffic could be
fatal. His brother, Sakurao, used to take him, but when Sakurao
got a job at a pharmaceutical company and moved into an em-
ployees' dormitory, his father began going with Hikari. His mother
escorted him while his father was in America.

The fifty workers at the center are all mentally handicapped;
some have Down's syndrome, some are autistic. Hikari is mildly
retarded (that is, having an IQ in the range of 55–70 and a mental
age of 8–12), but his autism compounds many of the problems involved. In the mornings, he and his colleagues do tasks like cleaning parks or making simple objects, such as woven scarves, and are
paid for what they do. His first job there was putting disposable

chopsticks—the kind used in many restaurants—in their narrow paper envelopes. Now, Hikari mostly assembles clothespins, using a device that resembles a stapler. He is a slow worker; his colleagues average $90 a month, but owing partly to his time-consuming penchant for arranging his clothespins in beautiful patterns on the table, he earns only about $11. (He used to give most of it to Sakurao for escorting him every day.) In the afternoons, the workers at the center are given lessons in useful skills like cooking or pleasurable ones like music, which is, of course, what Hikari most enjoys.

But his attendance at the center did not put an end to Ms. Tamura's music lessons. A scene in a television documentary later provided a glimpse of her contributing, along with Hikari's parents, to the evolution of one of Hikari's compositions. She pointed out that the piece changes from a major to a minor key in a section called "The Road Home." "Maybe the sun is setting," Yukari said. Kenzaburo noticed that the section that refers to a trip to Hiroshima also has a sad feeling. "So, one minor key," Hikari says. "I see," his father replies, "a minor key for Hiroshima. You've thought it out."

As Hikari matured as a composer, Ms. Tamura began to find her knowledge was not always sufficient to guide him when difficulties arose. She needed to turn for advice to her own former teacher, a retired professor from the Tokyo National University of Fine Arts and Music who had taught Baroque music there and who still teaches a few private students. And Hikari, seeing himself outgrowing his teacher, started to realize something about the progress he had made.

Kenzaburo has written in various places about incidents that he believes reflect Hikari's growing consciousness of having attained greater dignity through his musical skills, and perhaps even of having a self. Hikari went off on a required school trip to spend some time living in a dorm with his fellow students. Before he left, late one night when Kenzaburo stopped by his room to see if he was all right, Hikari asked, "Can't you sleep? Will you be able to sleep while I'm away? Cheer up—and get some sleep!" The day he came home, Yukari knocked herself out cooking all his favorite foods for dinner. When the meal was ready, his father called him to come eat, using his nickname, Pooh. He did not come. He didn't even answer. Finally, he told his family, "Pooh can't come. Pooh doesn't exist anymore." Sakurao speculated that, now that he had been functioning away from his family for a while and was about to come of age, Hikari might have decided he had outgrown his childhood nickname. "Come on, Hikari," he called. "Let's eat now. Mom has made so many dishes for you." It worked; Hikari said, "Yes, let's eat," and finally joined his family at the table.

These days, though, he no longer needs to assert his dignity by rejecting his childish nickname, which his mother said she thought he did only because a teacher who misunderstood it had told him it was unsuitable. In any case, he is now happy to answer, among the family, to the name of Pooh—a character who, as readers of Milne's books will recall, was greatly loved, enjoyed composing "hums," and sometimes proved wiser than he seemed.

Coming of Age

Twenty is the age of majority in Japan, and Hikari's coming-of-age year, 1983, was an eventful one; in fact, it was the start of the period when he began to come into his own. First, Kenzaburo wrote a book in which Hikari appeared directly, not as the inspiration for a fictional character but as himself, and this book, which proved to be quite popular, introduced him to the Japanese public in his own right. Kenzaburo called it *Rise Up, O Young Men of the New Age* and said it was inspired partly by becoming aware of the need to prepare Hikari for life after his father's death. In this book, narratives about Hikari, partly factual, partly fictional, are interleaved with material inspired by the author's close study of the eighteenth-century English visionary poet and artist William Blake (the source of the title).

Kenzaburo says that getting Hikari's particular voice right was the most important challenge he met in writing this book. "Hikari's dialogue there is almost entirely composed of things he actually said, although I had to rearrange them," he explains. "I began writing it by creating short stories based on his remarks. When he said something interesting in real life, I began to think about using this dialogue. And whenever I wrote a story around it, always, when I was trying to find the core of the story, I would find it in something Hikari had actually said."

In 1997, he spoke about this in public with John Nathan, the translator of *A Personal Matter* and the *Teach Us to Outgrow Our Madness* collection, who was in the middle of translating *Rise Up*. Kenzaburo said, "My son's way of speaking is very simple, sometimes awkward, but at the same time always very genuine and clear and sometimes very funny." And Professor Nathan described the problems he encountered in trying to recreate Hikari's speech in another language. "It's a subtly unnerving voice," he said. "It seems like a bright, intelligent voice, but there is nothing beneath the surface."

Kenzaburo says he doesn't invent Hikari's dialogue because he *couldn't:* "He has a distinct style of his own, and it's very funny. I would say the way he speaks is traditional and polite, and it's also very keen. He uses the kind of formal, old-fashioned Japanese that was spoken by my parents. Journalists in Japan have commented that our family has a very polite and old-fashioned way of talking. And my wife's family also talked that way. Mansaku Itami always spoke very politely and traditionally, and that's the way we speak in my family. Hikari seems especially intrigued by that style of speech. I think he's attracted by it because the announcers for classical-music programs speak that way.

"He uses a very soft voice, and speaks very slowly. It's a very cordial way of speaking. When I phone Japan, he always answers very quietly, and I really like it. In almost every family in Japan today, the young men speak much more informally, but the children in my family don't speak familiarly. I think they take their tone from Hikari's style. He sounds very aristocratic, very cultured. Not like a courtier, but like the servant of a courtier, maybe."

Before the publication of this book, the Japanese public was aware that Kenzaburo Oe had a brain-damaged son, and that many of the author's characters were somehow based on this child. Once the book came out, many real details of Hikari's life became common knowledge. Some of them—such as accounts of his aggressive and even violent behavior toward his mother and siblings—are painful; while Kenzaburo is characteristically concerned to interpret Hikari's motives constructively, his behavior is by no means idealized.

In addition to its humorous representations of Hikari's way of talking and its unsparing depictions of his bad behavior, the book deals with Hikari's great fear of death—a subject Kenzaburo has often addressed—and wariness about doing anything he perceives to be dangerous. It opens with an account of Hikari's cautious attempts at swimming. Before he graduated from school, his father decided that he might be ready to learn another skill, having gained so much self-confidence from his success with music, and tried to teach him to swim at a private club—a club that found its way into a good deal of his fiction.

The swimming teacher at Hikari's special school had given up on him, saying he seemed to have no intention of learning. Kenzaburo began his lessons by taking him to the shallow end of the pool, and Hikari tried to do what his father told him to there, but he moved so slowly that he couldn't swim properly. Whenever he began sinking, he would simply put his feet on the floor of the pool and take a step before trying to swim again, eventually reaching the other side of the pool by repeating this sequence over and over. Hikari himself seemed to believe that this was swimming.

"It was a very charming style of swimming," his father said. "He moved so slowly and lightly, like a feather on the water. I loved to watch him." Kenzaburo took him to the club for these unorthodox swimming sessions for about two years.

One of the pools at this club was for members only, and it was often the only one Hikari could use, because the others were too crowded for his inefficient methods. In one of the fictional portions of *Rise Up,* this pool, which was enclosed within glass walls, is taken over by a bizarre group of political extremists who seem to belong to a reactionary militarist cult similar to the one the novelist Yukio Mishima had led at the time of his legendary failed coup and spectacular suicide. They try to speak in Spanish, presumably in preparation for settling in Mexico; they have plans to emigrate there. When they occupy the pool, Hikari has no place to swim. Their leader criticizes Kenzaburo for spoiling Hikari and says he should discipline him more.

On the day of the tenth anniversary of Mishima's death, November 25, 1980, the group can be expected to do something disruptive; such groups often mark the anniversary of Mishima's death with rallies and mass meetings that sometimes get out of hand. They are in possession of the pool. Kenzaburo is sitting outside its glass walls on a bench with Hikari, waiting for their turn to go in. Suddenly one of the group members breaks the glass and begins shouting Spanish words: "Child! Boy! Pool! Difficult! Bad! Dangerous! Drown!"† And Kenzaburo abruptly realizes that Hikari is no longer sitting on the bench beside him. (Kenzaburo said that many people mistook this account for something factual and criticized him for having allowed his attention to wander, leaving Hikari in a dangerous situation, something he insisted would never happen in

†The dagger here, and throughout the chapter, follows translations by Yoshiko Kuwahara.

60

real life.) The leader of the group, who has been presented as a sinister figure, runs by, leaps into the deep diving pool where Hikari is drowning, and fishes him out. The man says to Kenzaburo, "It's difficult to take care of children, isn't it? But we can't quit being parents once we begin, can we?"† Kenzaburo is amazed; this is so unlike everything this man has previously said. And when Kenzaburo asks Hikari if he is all right, Hikari, to Kenzaburo's further surprise, says cheerfully, "I'm fine! I drowned. But from now on I will swim. It's time I learned."† In fact, Kenzaburo said, everyone at the club had always been very kind to Hikari and considerate of his special needs.

Poignantly, this book, which describes Hikari in darker terms than any other his father has written, is the only one of Kenzaburo's works that Hikari has actually read. His reading skills are limited, and he is not much interested in reading about anything but music. While some of Kenzaburo's writing is quite straightforward and accessible, some, especially his later fiction, is notorious for the difficulty of its style. Critics in Japan have complained that his prose sometimes reads like translations from European languages. What does Hikari know about his role in his father's work?

Kenzaburo says that Hikari has read a little of what he has written about him and about characters somehow based on him. "He knows that I have used him for characters in my work, and I believe he is proud to have been part of the characters he likes so much. He believes that he creates his music alone but that I am creating my work *with him*.

"He knows that he is Eeyore besides being Hikari and Pooh. The books where he has the most important roles are 'The Waters Have Come in Unto My Soul,' 'Rise Up, O Young Men of the New Age,' and 'A Personal Matter.' He knows about them, but the only one he has really read is 'Rise Up, O Young Men of the New Age.' His words are printed in a different typeface there, so he can find them easily. I did that on purpose. And it makes him very happy to read it. He says, 'This is my dialogue.' And he remembers exactly what he really said, and gets very angry if I didn't quote it correctly. So I *must* use things he really said. That's why I have to write truly about him!"

In real life, Hikari is very gentle and shy. Yet Kenzaburo's book describes episodes of violence he had in his teens, which his father says were entirely factual. The first occurred while Kenzaburo was in Europe. Hikari was playing hide-and-seek with his mother and other mothers and students from his special school. When his mother ran away from him with the other mothers—as part of the game—he got very upset and thrust out his leg in her path, tripping her so that she fell and bled from a head wound. She could not get up for a while and in fact had a concussion.

Mentally, Hikari was still a child. And like any child, he would surely have experienced his father's prolonged absence as a desertion. And if normal children have "separation anxiety" under such circumstances, imagine the galvanic distress someone as dependent as Hikari must experience when, in his father's absence, he sees his mother running away from him. His father believes he also experienced terrific anxiety about his epilepsy. He hadn't had much time to get used to it, and he could not really understand what it meant. After all, it is a heavy affliction even for a rational adult who can understand what a seizure is, and means. For someone with Hikari's mental limitations, epileptic seizures must be particularly horrific.

Whether because his father's absence aggravated the anxieties caused by his epilepsy or for some purely physical reason, his violent behavior continued. Later that day, he bullied Sakurao, too, holding him in a full nelson and poking him. On another occasion, he got irritated at Natsumiko's solicitude and punched her in the face. His siblings—and Yukari, too—began to be afraid of him and kept their distance. Hikari retaliated by turning his tape recorder up to full volume and keeping it that way all day.

Another evening, at dinnertime, Hikari, who is not supposed

to handle anything sharp because of his poor coordination, grabbed a kitchen knife and stood at the window with it, looking out at the dark garden while the rest of the family ate. Yukari began to think he might have to be hospitalized to prevent his hurting himself or anyone else. They had no way of controlling him if he became violent; in his father's absence, he was the biggest and strongest of them all. He and Kenzaburo were about equally matched, but Kenzaburo was not there.

When his father returned from his trip, he brought Hikari a harmonica, but he was sulky and refused to take any interest in it. And he glared angrily at Kenzaburo, but the violent behavior ceased.

Yukari told her husband that while he was away, she had tried to get their wayward child to pull himself together by telling him that when his father got home, she would have to tell him all about what Hikari had done. Hikari had said, "No, Dad is dead!"† No matter what Yukari said or how often she repeated that Kenzaburo would be back on Sunday, Hikari maintained that his father had died.

The morning after she told him about what Hikari had said, Kenzaburo, who was suffering from gout, was resting with his foot up on the sofa. Hikari gently touched it and asked whether his "good foot" was all right. Kenzaburo saw that his son's eyes were no longer angry. Hikari picked up the harmonica he had rejected and began to play a Bach siciliana. Kenzaburo decided that by calling his painful foot "good," Hikari was trying to perform a kind of magic, hoping to make it better by calling it "good."

Kenzaburo reasoned that Hikari's violence must have been a reaction to the realization that his father was mortal. Kenzaburo also wondered whether the evening when Hikari had faced the dark garden, clutching a knife while the family ate, had not been really a threat of violence against himself or them but rather a preparation for defending them against the outside world when his father was not there to do it. Yukari did not agree with his interpretation, but Kenzaburo decided that the hostile glare he had seen in Hikari's eyes expressed as much sorrow as anger. Apparently Hikari's difficult episodes are always followed by shamefaced repentance.

And Hikari is upset even to think he may have been tactless. Kenzaburo described Hikari's concern with problems of communication in *M/T*, another partly fictional, partly factual book that includes actual events from Hikari's twentieth year. This book was of even greater importance for Hikari than *Rise Up* had been, for it also includes a piece Hikari wrote then; Hikari's own hand-written manuscript, reproduced in the book, was his first published composition.

In *M/T,* Kenzaburo tells of taking his whole family to visit his mother in Shikoku. In the airplane on their way back to Tokyo, Natsumiko tells her mother what Hikari said to his grandmother by way of good-bye: "Keep well, and have a good death!" Natsumiko says the old lady replied, "Yes, I will keep well, and I will have a good death. But, Hikari, I will miss you." Natsumiko adds that she doesn't think that what Hikari said was very polite.

Sakurao suggests that what Hikari must have meant was that his grandmother should stay well as long as she was alive, and that when she could live no longer—well, she couldn't be expected to stay healthy after she was dead, could she? Hikari must have meant that she should stay well for the rest of her life. Natsumiko finally asks her elder brother, who is sitting by himself watching the clouds out the window. After speaking to him for a while, she returns to the others. "He says Sakurao is right. But he wants to call Grandmother and apologize for having expressed himself badly. What he actually meant to say—Hey, Hikari, what was it you wanted to say?"

"Keep well and live well!" Hikari bellows, startling the other passengers. "I'm sorry, and I'll correct it on the phone," he says, with a smile.

But once the family are back in Tokyo, Hikari becomes obsessed with the idea of returning to Shikoku alone to visit his grandmother. "I said something unfortunate. I corrected it on the phone, but is that really enough? How can I be sure Grandmother understood? Since she's getting deaf, I'm very worried about that!" His parents finally agree to let him go on an airplane by himself, arranging for his aunt, who still lives near her mother in Shikoku, to pick him up when he arrives.

His grandmother is mostly bedridden by this time. Hikari spends his days stretched out on the floor by her bed, listening to classical music on FM radio, and at the times of day when no classical music is broadcast, his grandmother tells him the local legends, just as her mother, Kenzaburo's grandmother, had told them to Kenzaburo when he was a boy. Some of them concern the founder of the valley community, known as "The Destroyer," although his destructive acts, such as the dynamiting of a rock that blocked the early settlers' way, tended to have constructive purposes. And Hikari, hearing her tales, is inspired to write a piece of music called "The Destroyer," subtitled "Forest Ballad."

Kenzaburo sends her a tape of the piece, and she writes him a letter saying that when Hikari visited her, she was afraid she had bored him by nattering on about the legends of the old days, but after hearing this tape, she knows Hikari understands the legends she told him, because she can recognize the music; it's music she heard in the forest when she was young.

M/T, which primarily concerns these legends of the valley in Shikoku—the letters stand for Matriarch and Trickster, archetypes that recur in the tales—is part fact, part adapted myth, and part fiction. Hikari really did tell his grandmother to have a good death, and brooded about having done so, but in real life his parents would never dream of letting him go to Shikoku by himself. His grandmother had told him some local legends while the whole family was staying at her house. And he did write "The Destroyer," inspired by these stories; her reaction, when Kenzaburo sent her a tape of it, was faithfully recorded in his book.

"She *is* a storyteller, but I almost believed it was true—or believed it was almost true—when she said she knew that music," Kenzaburo now says. "We didn't ask her, What instrument did you hear in the forest, in the old days?"

His mother had always had an eccentric way of pretending she was never surprised because she knew everything already. To the news of Kenzaburo's early literary successes, Hikari's birth and abnormalities, and the discovery of his musical abilities, her reaction was invariably, "I knew it. Your father knew it." She claimed her late husband had had a great big book where he read accounts of the family's future, and Kenzaburo has said he believes he can trace the beginning of his literary career to this factitious book. He said he started reading literature in foreign languages hoping to find it, figuring anything so wondrous and magical couldn't be written in the language he spoke every day; then, when he realized the book didn't exist, trying to write something like it himself. So she claimed to have known in advance that Hikari would someday write music she would recognize as part of the legends she had grown up with. "It sounds like a joke," Kenzaburo says, "but when she talks about Hikari's music, I believe she always speaks very sincerely."

M/T was published in 1986, when Hikari was twenty-three. It was the Japanese public's introduction to his music. Tens of thousands of readers could see Hikari's painstaking, wobbly, childish-looking notation for themselves; those who knew how could sight-read it in their heads; some sat down and played it on a piano. And at least one reader—one who was later to transform Hikari's life—was fascinated enough to take the trouble to copy it out on standard-size music paper before doing so.

The following year Kenzaburo published more of Hikari's music, privately. *Hikari Oe Pieces for Piano* was an edition of two hundred copies of scores of the sixteen pieces the family and Ms. Tamura considered Hikari's best. Kenzaburo has written that each of the pieces conjured up memories of specific scenes of family life for him, but he shared the scores with very few people outside the family's intimate circle.

Kenzaburo had many highly influential friends in Japan's musical world. The most eminent was Toru Takemitsu, who was not only aware that Hikari had extraordinary musical abilities but had sometimes enjoyed playing musical games with him. Shortly before Hikari turned twenty, Takemitsu visited the Oes' summer house in North Karuizawa with John Cage; they were both participating in a music festival in the area. Takemitsu was showing off Hikari's abilities to Cage, who got caught up in tapping glasses with knives, marveling at Hikari's unfailingly correct identification of the tones he produced. At first, Hikari played along patiently, but finally getting bored, he gave Cage a hard look and a counterchallenge, rapping on an apple and inviting Cage to identify the pitch. (Cage was also bent on showing off his mycological expertise, gathering local mushrooms and asking Yukari to cook them. Kenzaburo advised her not to, fearing that Japanese fungi might differ in subtle ways from the North American varieties Cage knew. Takemitsu, however, sautéed and ate some of Cage's offerings—and got high; the mushrooms proved to be a mildly psychedelic variety.)

Another prominent composer, Toshi Ichiyanagi, was close to the family, too. And Kenzaburo had been the first reporter in Japan to interview Seiji Ozawa, now the music director of the Boston Symphony Orchestra and still a neighbor of the Oes; he subsequently became a good friend. Their circle also included several high-profile performers. Shomura Kiyoshi, one of Japan's best-known guitarists, is Yukari's first cousin, the son of her father's younger sister.

But Kenzaburo didn't want to impose on them or take advantage of their friendship. "I didn't think professional musicians would have any real interest in it, anyway. So I only distributed twenty or thirty copies," he said. "They were given to teachers at

Hikari's school, and to a few friends of the family. The rest stayed under my bed for years."

He had, however, given the scores to one professional musician, the pianist Akiko Ebi, a family friend with a distinguished career, who had won several international competitions. She played the pieces and made a tape that she sent the Oes from France, where she was working at the time. It arrived on Christmas eve, and the Oes popped it into their machine at once. "That was the best Christmas of our lives," Kenzaburo said. "Hearing this music was an extraordinary experience. You cannot imagine the effect it had on us. We were surprised, stupefied. We had never heard Hikari's music played by such an artist before, and we had not realized the quality of his musical expression."

Hikari's parents had known, of course, that their son had some extraordinary musical abilities. Perfect pitch was the least of it. His musical memory was downright uncanny: he could hear a few measures of Mozart and immediately identify the piece they came from by its Köchel number—the number that follows the letter K after each of Mozart's works, according to a chronological catalogue first made by a nineteenth-century musicologist. There are over six hundred of them, and even professional Mozart experts are unlikely to know—much less come up with after hearing a few bars—a majority of such a vast catalogue.

Beginning to realize now how far their son's musical brilliance went beyond such memory stunts, Kenzaburo and Yukari began to wonder where his talent came from. "There was no musical ability at all on my side of the family," Kenzaburo admits flatly. For generations, his family had supervised the stripping and pulping of tree bark. His older brother, now dead, had worked for the forestry service, too, doing manual labor to finance Kenzaburo's education. His sister is a housewife, with no musical hobbies; his younger brother is a police detective with no interest in any of the arts. His mother likes songs, but Kenzaburo says he would hardly call her "musical." His father may have studied music, though; Kenzaburo can remember him coming out with scraps of far-reaching knowledge about both Asian and European arts.

Kenzaburo denies having any musical ability himself and enjoys illustrating this assertion by telling the story of his own brief foray into the world of song. His stint in a school glee club ended in disgrace when he could not reach an A he was supposed to sing—something by Massenet, as he recalls—and his classmates teased him for a while by calling him "O," since he had dropped the other letter in his name, the E being pronounced with the sound of a long A. In fact, he has a pleasant, resonant baritone. ("Hikari doesn't like my singing, though," he says.) And he talks knowledgeably and feelingly about both Japanese and Western music. Apart from his friendships with a number of Japan's most stellar composers and performers, many musical works themselves seem to be important points of reference to him in almost the same way literary works are; he mentions Bach's Mass in B Minor, for example, or *La Traviata* to clarify what he is saying.

Yukari's mother's family, the Nodas, on the other hand, were an old samurai family with no professional musicians among them but many keen and talented amateurs. Her mother's sister gained some fame for playing the koto (a zitherlike Japanese instrument), and one of Yukari's mother's older brothers played the biwa (another Japanese instrument, which resembles a lute). Another older brother, Minoru, a naval officer who had studied in Europe, played the violin. Sometime around 1910, he composed several operettas in the style of Offenbach, which were performed by students. He was a close friend of Yukari's father's when they were in middle school; it was mostly their common interest in music that brought them together. Sadly, he died of tuberculosis when he was only in his thirties. Yukari said that one of his songs, a light piece in Western classical style, sounds like something Hikari might have written.

Yukari's mother, Kimi, always enjoyed singing, and even now, at ninety-three, can remember the lyrics to most of the songs she knows, despite some senile dementia that led, when she lived with Kenzaburo and Yukari at times in the nineteen-eighties, to the erratic behavior he describes in an essay in *A Healing Family*. Yukari's father was very fond of Western classical music, played the violin very well, and composed some of the music for the films he directed, including one particularly successful number—created for a bunch of bandits to sing in their hideout—in the style of a folk song. Shomura, the guitarist mentioned above, is Yukari's cousin on his side. It seems plain that if Hikari's musicality has some inherited components, they come from his mother's side of the family. ("That's where Hikari's good looks come from, too," Kenzaburo graciously adds.)

Wherever it came from, Hikari's music had already been launched on the path that would take it to an enormous global audience. On one occasion, when Kenzaburo had gone abroad for a stint as a research associate at the University of California, Berkeley, Hikari went through a spell of disobedience; despite the mutually supportive strength of Yukari, Natsumiko, and Sakurao, his dependence on his father is so great that problems of that kind almost invariably arise whenever Kenzaburo is gone for more than a few days. Yukari urged Kenzaburo to try to talk some sense into him over the telephone, and Kenzaburo scolded him, insisting on better behavior. Ten days later, Kenzaburo received a gloomily repentant letter in which Hikari said, "I should never have lived to be twenty." It's a poignantly ironic number to have named, since it was a piece of music he wrote in the year he came of age that led the world to discover his talent.

Kenzaburo and Yukari Oe had been told that their first child, Hikari, born brain-damaged and autistic, could never learn to speak; doctors had advised them to let the baby die. Kenzaburo wrote an internationally successful novel, "A Personal Matter," concerning that experience. Because of Hikari's special needs, caring for him was particularly difficult, and physically exhausting, yet his parents refused to give up on him, showering him with affection and persistently trying to discover a key that would unlock his silence.

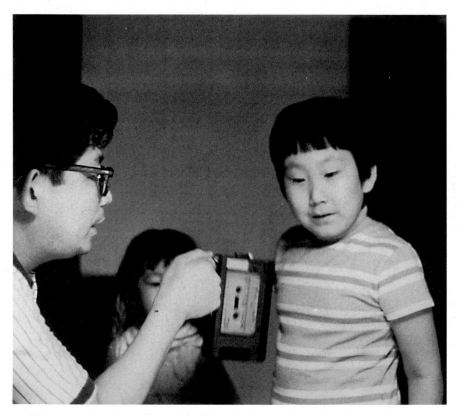

His parents' patient effort paid off: suddenly one day, when he was six years old, Hikari proved that he was capable of speech after all. After that, the Oes tried every means possible to get him to talk; here, Kenzaburo is coaxing his son to speak into a tape recorder. Hikari's sister, Natsumiko, is behind them.

Hikari started taking classes in a Tokyo special-education facility when he was eight years old; this picture was taken on his first day of school. By then it was clear that he had unusual musical abilities; he spent all his spare time listening to classical music; and he could correctly identify every piece he'd ever heard. The following year, his mother began teaching him to play the piano.

When he was eleven, Hikari began piano lessons with Kumiko Tamura, who taught him notation. Soon he had transcribed something from every record the Oes owned, and when his teacher first saw unfamiliar passages in his notebooks, she thought they were transcriptions of pieces she didn't know. In fact, Hikari had begun composing: he completed his first finished piece at the age of thirteen.

ミスタープレリュード mister Prelude

アレグロ。

In 1992, when Hikari was twenty-nine, the first CD of his compositions was a smash success, breaking sales records in the classical category. His second CD, released in September 1994, was similarly successful. The following month, his father, who had continued writing about characters based on Hikari, won the Nobel Prize for literature. Here, father and son are looking together at the liner notes of Hikari's second CD.

Juzo Itami, one of Japan's most famous movie directors, is Hikari's uncle; he is Yukari's brother and was Kenzaburo's best friend in high school. He is shown here with Hikari on the set of "A Quiet Life," the film he made in 1995 based on Kenzaburo's novel. Its award-winning soundtrack features Hikari's compositions.

Kenzaburo and Hikari have a uniquely interdependent relationship; they have done much of their respective creative work together in this room. Once Hikari was clearly established as a successful composer, Kenzaburo announced that he was going to stop writing fiction, because his primary motivation for years had been the need to give his son a voice, and Hikari had triumphantly found a voice of his own. Fortunately, Kenzaburo later modified his decision: he would only give up writing fiction *about Hikari*. Kenzaburo is now working on a new novel.

Father and son were both world famous by 1996, when Kenzaburo came to America to teach at Princeton University. Hikari and Yukari joined Kenzaburo for public appearances at concerts of Hikari's music and readings of "A Healing Family," Kenzaburo's essays about their family life, which Yukari illustrated. Hikari missed his sister, who had stayed in Tokyo, but kept in touch by fax. He sent her this illustrated account of his musical and culinary experiences in New York City.

"A Quiet Life"

As Hikari reached his early twenties, his sister became involved in volunteer work with the handicapped. Using what she had learned from such activities, she could sometimes communicate with Hikari better than Kenzaburo and Yukari could. Kenzaburo wrote not only about their deepening relationship but also about whether he was exploiting them by using them in his fiction. His novel *A Quiet Life,* published in 1990, takes place in 1987, when Hikari was twenty-four. It is fiction, but while certain sensational episodes are pure invention, Kenzaburo has said that many of its less strenuously eventful moments were faithfully drawn from real life. Hikari, as himself and under his own name, is a major character, as are his brother and sister, who do not appear under their own names but are presented in some ways as themselves.

In 1995, his uncle Juzo Itami directed a movie based on it, with Hikari's compositions on the soundtrack; the CD won a prize. So Hikari has not only seen himself on television but has seen—and recognized—himself played by an actor in a film, as well. (Kenzaburo, in talking about the actors in this movie, did not describe them as playing this or that character but as playing himself, his wife, his daughter, and so on.) On top of that, the film, both in the version shown in theaters and in the video released for home viewing, has a documentary coda showing the real Kenzaburo, Yukari, and Hikari, where Hikari is, among other things, put in the odd and piquant position of being asked to comment on the performance of the actor who incarnates his father's representation of himself.

Hikari's response was, "He had a really great hat." This could be read—and almost has to be appreciated—as a witty, sophisticated putdown, but it is impossible to know what was going on in Hikari's mind. (He gave a whoop of laughter when his mother talked about his having said this, seeming proud rather than embarrassed; this does seem to suggest that his reply was consciously intended as a joke. His father says he is certain it was, adding that the actor sent Hikari the hat he had admired, which Hikari enjoyed wearing from time to time.)

One of the few things that experts on autism agree about is that the syndrome involves a defect in perception of one's own selfhood and, in consequence, that of others—a difficulty in distinguishing "you" from "I." Oliver Sacks has written that "appreciating other people for their otherness may be the most difficult achievement of all for an autistic person." The footage show-

ing the real Hikari includes a scene where he is watching the filming on a video monitor on the set. He nudges his mother and says,
"That's me!" He is giggling and looks self-consciously proud and
delighted. One can only speculate about what he may have been
experiencing—or recognizing—at that moment. Anybody might
find his notions of selfhood slipping and sliding under such circumstances; autism apart, the fact that his father has been creating
other versions of Hikari from the moment he was born must surely
have complicated his notions of "me." "He knows he is Eeyore,"
Kenzaburo says.

Has Hikari's privacy been violated by his father's representations of him? Both the novel and the movie versions of *A Quiet Life*
deal with his sexuality, a subject he might wish to keep private, and
the novel even deals with his losing control of his bowels during his
epileptic seizures. Asked if he had been embarrassed by certain
scenes in the movie, his mother said, "Not really. He was pleased to
see himself in the film." The concept of privacy is so bound up with
that of selfhood that it may be in some way inaccessible to the
autistic. For that matter, it is a relatively new concept in Japan.
There is no word for "privacy" in the Japanese language, because
the concept does not exist in traditional Japanese culture. Since
contact with the West introduced the idea, the English word has
been used, and the notion itself is as obviously exotic as the borrowed word. Of course, a writer can hardly be said in any culture
to violate his own privacy. But what about his family's? Most fiction incorporates at least some autobiographical elements, and
they are often fairly easy to spot, and much fiction contains at least
one character with a recognizable real-life model. In Kenzaburo
Oe's case, the fictionalizing process is open to the reader's inspec-
tion to an unusual degree, and the questions raised above come frequently to mind, partly because many of the circumstances of his
private life are public knowledge, partly because his fictionaliza-
tions are often highly fantastic (so that the boundary between the
real and the imagined is obvious), and partly because he has re-

turned almost obsessively to the same factual jumping-off places in book after book. Ever since *A Personal Matter* fictionalized the problems surrounding Hikari's birth, he has been showing the world that seemingly personal matters are public concerns.

Like *A Personal Matter*, *A Quiet Life* explores the dangers of heartless narcissism, the later novel by dramatizing the sufferings the members of a writer's family may undergo when they are co-opted in literature. "Our family situation," its twenty-year-old narrator-heroine Ma-chan tells the reader, "is to some extent publicly known from what Father writes." The family in question is an unmistakable version of the Oes, presented from the point of view of the only daughter: the father, known here only as K, is the author of some of Kenzaburo Oe's works; the mother, like Yukari, is the daughter of one famous film director and the sister of another; the oldest son is a brain-damaged composer whose name is Hikari, though he is usually referred to as Eeyore; the daughter, Ma-chan, is a French major in college (Natsumiko graduated from Sophia University with a degree in Japanese literature) and does volunteer work with the handicapped, as Natsumiko did as a student; the younger son, O-chan, is studying for college-entrance exams that will admit him to the Science Department of Tokyo University, from which Sakurao has since graduated. Even Hikari's piano teacher Kumiko Tamura makes an appearance here, as Mrs. T.

The role of the Hikari character in this novel is quite different from that of previous books. Before *Rise Up*, the character was a child. In *Rise Up*, the character, who has just left adolescence, is not really a fictional character at all but a real character in what are largely memoirs of real events, augmented with a few fictitious narratives. In *A Quiet Life*, the character is presented as though he were the real Hikari—and identified as such—but he is involved in events that, while not exactly fantastic, are very melodramatic indeed. The most striking impression one receives of life with Hikari from reading this novel, though, is how vulnerable his liability to epileptic seizures makes him, and how some family member must watch over him constantly.

Rise Up is even discussed in *A Quiet Life*. Ma-chan says, "Characters based on me and O-chan are portrayed. . . . So I said to O-chan, 'A pain in the neck, don't you think, even if it's been done favorably, that he writes about us from his one-dimensional viewpoint? It's all right with my friends who know me, but it depresses me to think that I'm going to meet some people who, through his stories, will have preconceived ideas of me.' 'Just tell them it's fiction,' the cool-headed O-chan replied."

Yukari, asked about the way her husband used family members to create characters, says, "Oh, well, it's fiction, so I don't really take it to heart. But sometimes people ask if this or that episode really happened—even about totally outrageous fictional events. Sometimes other authors' wives, who should know better. That does bother me—but, you know, it doesn't really bother me that much. Most of the people I see now are close friends, who know better, or people I know through Hikari's occupational center, and I've never actually had bad experiences because people thought my husband's fiction was true."

Natsumiko Oe has always guarded her privacy carefully, probably because of the ways she suffered for her father's fame and her brother's oddity when she was small. She never talks to reporters and declined to contribute any of her memories or thoughts about her brother to this book. Asked how Natsumiko felt about *A Quiet Life,* Kenzaburo said, "She doesn't speak about it publicly. She is very much her own person, very reserved, and not the kind of person who would communicate with just anybody. In that way, she is sort of a difficult person. She is a gentle girl, but she has her own ideas about things." Drawings she has done suggest that she has a well-developed and rather impish sense of humor, too: one whimsical creature, half-bird, half-human, resembles Edward Lear's fanciful life forms, though its style is more finished.

At the time *A Quiet Life* takes place, Natsumiko was actually doing volunteer work with the handicapped, having joined a social-service club at her university; she felt that her special protective relationship with Hikari had prepared her well for this work. (Such activities are rare for Japanese students, but Sophia, as a Catholic university, encourages them.) She worked mostly at a famous facility in western Japan for severely handicapped children of elementary-school age. There are very few institutions of that kind in the country, and this one is known as the best, so that parents of extremely handicapped children will move to Nagano to qualify for its benefits. The children there need total, twenty-four-hour care; they are so severely disabled that they not only can't feed themselves but can't chew their food; whoever is feeding them must push every spoonful far down their throats to be sure it is swallowed, watching vigilantly to be sure they don't choke. The school includes a dormitory, so that parents obliged to be away from home overnight can leave their children there for a small fee. Volunteers stay in this dormitory, watching the children all night, relieving each other in shifts; Natsumiko did this during her four years as an undergraduate.

Having originally joined the program because her experience with Hikari had given her insight into the needs of the handicapped, she found that her experience with these children helped her find new ways to understand Hikari. "Natsumiko was the first one to figure out the best ways to communicate with Hikari," Yukari says. "Even now, he often won't answer a direct question the first time it's put to him, but if you keep asking the same question in different ways, he'll eventually answer. Natsumiko is very resourceful in talking to him. When he doesn't answer a question, she'll think of things like asking, 'Who understands the question I just asked?' to get an answer. I think I understand his personality, but Natsumiko is much better at coaxing him out of a really bad mood than I am. She'll get him to talk about what he's been hearing on the radio until he's in a better frame of mind. When he's in a bad mood, it usually turns out to be because he isn't feeling well physically.

"Sometimes he gets very frustrated if he has some health problem and knows he needs help but doesn't know how to begin explaining what's wrong. When his stomach is bothering him, for
example, he will ask me or Natsumiko, 'Does your stomach hurt?'
I used to think he was asking me because I looked somehow as if I
had a stomachache, but Natsumiko figured out that he was asking
because his own stomach hurt and he couldn't say so directly. She's
always teaching us how to communicate better with him."

A Quiet Life is, in part, an exploration—and in some ways a celebration—of Natsumiko's relationship with Hikari. Inevitably, it's
also an exposure. Kenzaburo always speaks very respectfully of his
daughter's wish for privacy, which he sees as part of her indepen-
dence. But it would not be altogether unfair to describe *A Quiet Life*
as one long intrusion. The title—derived from Ma-chan's avowed
ambition—is largely ironic, for the book begins and ends with sensational sexual assaults. And it is plain that life can be only so quiet
in a family whose head is not only a public figure but also to some
extent famous precisely because he has exposed so much of his private life to public view. The intervening chapters, on the other
hand, are quiet enough. They consist mostly of discussions of several books and one movie; a description of a family funeral; reports
of conversations with Eeyore's music teacher, an eccentric specialist
in eastern European literature and his paradoxically unusual wife, a
proudly self-declared "nobody"; and accounts—which are all the
more moving for their simple straightforwardness—of the pains
and pleasures of family life with a retarded man.

No short plot summary could do justice to the novel's com-
plexities, but an outline will indicate the extent to which it hinges
on questions about whether the father's writing has been harmful
to his family. In the book, Ma-chan is left in charge of the house-
hold when K leaves for a stint at the University of California,
Berkeley—as Kenzaburo actually did in real life—and Mother
joins him there because he is suffering some sort of depressive crisis. Before leaving, Father suggested that Eeyore take up swim-

ming again, and Ma-chan has reason to think the exercise is supposed to deflect his sexual energies. The family, like the Oes actually, has been harassed by oddballs. When Ma-chan learns that
someone has been molesting little girls in their neighborhood, she
becomes afraid Eeyore might be the crinimal, but it turns out to be
one of the kooks; Kenzaburo's fame has brought him to the neighborhood and given him an excuse for lurking there. And when
Eeyore writes a very sad composition and gives it the title "Abandoned Child," everyone is inclined to blame K for going off to a
foreign country and summoning his wife to his side, leaving his
needy son abandoned.

Eeyore has an interest in death, which manifests itself much
like the real-life Hikari's. For one thing, the character is a devoted
obituary reader, bowing over the newspaper whenever he sees a
name he recognizes from music or sumo. When Eeyore flies to
Shikoku with his sister to attend their uncle's funeral, relatives
there become alarmed when Eeyore tells them the title of his latest
piece. Eventually, he tells his grandmother that the full title of the
piece is "Rescuing an Abandoned Child," and that it refers to an incident when his fellow workers at the welfare center discovered an
abandoned infant in the course of cleaning a park. He wishes he
could find one and rescue it, too; oddly, this is accepted unques-
tioningly as proving that he was not prompted to write the piece
by feeling like an abandoned child himself.

The last fifth of the novel is given over to a highly melodramatic plot whose main purpose seems to be to question the use
Kenzaburo Oe has made of his family in his fiction. Finally imple-
menting K's suggestion about Eeyore's swimming, Ma-chan
takes him to the club where he had swum with his father in the
past, and a man called Mr. Arai volunteers to coach him for free.
Eeyore enjoys and takes pride in swimming. Kenzaburo said that
Hikari was in fact swimming, as described, at the time the novel
takes place, but he himself was Hikari's coach during the two
years Hikari tried the sport. Kenzaburo has been a member of the

club where the swimming scenes take place for thirty-five years and is now one of its directors. He has set many scenes there, in various works such as *Rise Up* and *An Echo of Heaven*, and although people in his fiction do not always behave well to Hikari at that club, Kenzaburo says that in real life everyone there was always kind to his son.

When Ma-chan mentions Arai in passing in a letter to her father, he sends her a special-delivery letter telling her to make sure she is never, under any circumstances, alone with the man. Later, Arai beats up Eeyore's music teacher, and it comes out that the reason K didn't want his daughter to be alone with Arai is that he was the real-life model for a character in one of K's stories. The story, "Swimming Man," is one of Kenzaburo Oe's most famous. (No English translation exists as yet.) In that story, a young man murders a woman after sexually torturing her, and an older man decides to take the blame for this crime. In *A Quiet Life,* Arai is supposed to have sold his diary to K, who developed his story from the account he found there.

Arai contrives to trap Ma-chan in his apartment, with Eeyore shut into the apartment next door. Arai threatens Ma-chan with the kind of sexual torture used in "Swimming Man." Eeyore escapes and saves her, and next time Mother calls, Eeyore blurts out, "Ma-chan was in big trouble, but I fought!" Mother gets an explanation out of O-chan and promptly returns to Japan. Eeyore is allowed to have the last word, giving the book its title.

There is a kind of running gag about Eeyore: since his means of expression are so limited, the characters who surround him feel obliged to use their imaginations to supplement the information he provides about himself, just as Kenzaburo has written, in *A Healing Family,* that he and his wife and his other children all do in real life with Hikari. In *A Quiet Life,* everyone jumps to the worst conclusions, living in nearly perpetual alarm about him, yet their worries invariably prove unjustified. For example, the characters who misunderstand the "Abandoned Child" title seem all but ready to lynch Eeyore's father for abandoning him, and when Eeyore explains the reference, everyone is chagrined.

Yet the question of the absent father's guilt is never really resolved. In fact, the novel is in a way a long exploration of that question, and some of its most strongly felt passages condemn the claims of exceptional individuals to exceptional privileges. Sometimes K is seen as having failed Ma-chan and her younger brother O-chan by neglecting them through his devotion to their needier brother. K suffers from depression, and his friends and family often see his need to deal with his own mental and emotional state as irresponsible self-indulgence.

But his crimes are dramatized most sensationally in the framing sexual incidents. In the first, it is the father's fame that gives the child molester an excuse to hang around the family's neighborhood. And what is going on in the final episode? Is it a simple dramatization of the sort of thing that happened when, for example, Oe and his young wife were subjected to physical attacks by the outraged defenders of the character he skewered in "Seventeen"? But what kind of father would put his daughter in danger, however imaginary, of a revenge that includes sexual torture? Or is that the very question Oe wants us to ask, along with the characters who are so quick—and often so misguided—to condemn K?

In previous fiction, Kenzaburo had used fictionalized versions of himself and of other members of his family, especially Hikari, as characters; this one goes much further, being told from the point of view of a fictionalized version of his daughter (thus claiming to expose her inner life) and subjecting her—along with the Hikari character—to some very disturbing experiences. At the same time, it would also not be unfair to describe the book as Kenzaburo Oe's condemnation of himself for all his family has had to suffer, not only as a direct result of his literary work but from having to live with the personality that created it. Condemning oneself for what one is in the act of doing can, of course, be consciously preemptive, but in this case it seems more like yet another instance of Kenzaburo's consistently amazing honesty. He knows that his claiming to express the thoughts of others, both as a writer and as a father, is presumptuous and perhaps unforgivably so; he also knows that he cannot help continuing to make these claims, even though they may have destructive results and may, heartbreakingly, prove to have no validity at all.

The movie version follows the book's plot fairly faithfully. The major changes involve heightening the drama. Ma-chan's character is enormously sympathetic in the book and remains so in the film, but the way she is presented is considerably altered there. Her demeanor is demure in both versions, but in the novel she has a bold and truly independent mind, and more than her share of stubbornness, though her self-possession is always being scuttled by a self-doubt that leaves her collapsing into passivity—she calls it "robotizing"—when the going gets rough. She is a piquant mix of vulnerability and feistiness there, but in the movie—partly because her intellectual life has been excised—she seems far more vulnerable, fragile, innocent, and naive than in the book.

Atsuro Watabe, the actor who plays Hikari, appears to have studied his mannerisms diligently and has caught some of them to the life. Overall, though, his peculiarities are exaggerated—there's an awful lot of writhing and extreme tucking in of the chin to the chest. These exaggerations are not done offensively, though; Kenzaburo and Yukari both said they thought the actor's performance was very good.

In the documentary coda about the characters' real-life models, Juzo Itami introduces Kenzaburo, Yukari, and Hikari Oe, who are all shown watching "themselves" as they appear in the film on a video monitor. Perhaps the circumstances made him nervous, perhaps the film was edited selectively, perhaps Mr. Watabe's performance gave him ideas, but for whatever reason, when Hikari appears, he seems to be exaggerating his own peculiar mannerisms. In most of this footage, he looks far more extremely abnormal than he did either in television documentaries or in any of his appearances in America.

Juzo Itami and Nobuko Miyamoto—who, besides being his most famous star, is his wife, and so Hikari's aunt—are quite close to the Oes. Yukari said that they see them much more often than they see anyone on the Oe side of the family, since her husband's relatives live so far away, and that both of them are very fond of Hikari; Ms. Miyamoto visits him frequently, with Mr. Itami accompanying her as often as his busy schedule permits.

Mr. Itami told Yukari that the documentary portion of the film was very well received though the whole movie was a flop. Itami's movies are usually smash successes, and he ribbed Kenzaburo about its failure, saying that anything with his name on it was bound to do badly; in fact, continuing prejudice against the handicapped in Japan was probably responsible for its poor reception. It has an outstanding cast: Tsutomu Yamazaki, an eminent Shakespearean actor, plays K; Takao Okamura, a great operatic tenor, plays the music teacher; and the adorable Nobuko Miyamoto, internationally beloved for her performances in her husband's *Tampopo* and *Taxing Woman* movies, plays the music teacher's wife. Itami's pacing is bouncy and his comic touch is sure, but the film also—as Kenzaburo remarks in the documentary portion—achieves real pathos in a scene where, after Eeyore has defended Ma-chan from Arai's attack, brother and sister kneel outside on the ground, hugging each other in the rain. Perhaps it will have a warmer reception in foreign countries, which have received Itami's previous movies so enthusiastically; an English-subtitled version has been prepared, but the film has not yet been released outside Japan.

By the time the movie was made, Hikari was a celebrity in his own right, as a result of his own creations. But when Kenzaburo wrote the novel and gave it its ironic title, he had no way of guessing how soon the quietness (such as it was) of Hikari's life would be gone beyond recalling. And all his fretting about the harm his fame—and the writing that brought it—might have done to his family became largely irrelevant as Hikari attained a stardom that was entirely his own.

Sudden Success

In 1991, Kenzaburo published another collection of his son's scores, *Hikari Oe Pieces for Flute and Piano*. Meanwhile, one of the people who had read *M/T* and discovered Hikari's piece in it was thinking about producing a recording of Hikari's work. He was a young man a year older than Hikari called Hiroyuki Okano, a longtime fan of Kenzaburo's books. He was also the new head of

THE MUSIC OF LIGHT

the Western-music division of the Nippon Columbia record company. He had been a philosophy major in college, concentrating on aesthetics, and had chosen a career in music after giving up a job at IBM to find something more meaningful. After reading *M/T,* he copied out Hikari's score himself and played it on the piano; the strong, visceral reaction he had to it then ("It was shocking . . . such deep emotions,"* he said) inspired him to ask Kenzaburo what else his son had written, soon persuading the author to haul a copy of the scores out from under his bed and to introduce him to Akiko Ebi. He was struck by the consistency of Hikari's musical sensitivity, especially in his choices of keys, and he found Hikari's straightforward titles refreshing. The idea of producing a CD of Hikari's work became his pet project.

He told a reporter later that at that time, "the bubble economy was in full swing, CDs had really begun to take off because company-sponsored concerts had started proliferating, and I felt that something was being lost in the deluge of sound that resulted. When I thought about what I wanted to do as Classical Music Director, Hikari's music was what came to mind. I got to feeling very happy. Isn't this what living is all about—music like this? . . . Hikari's emotional experience of life is directly expressed in his music. I think people are enchanted by this. Moreover, I think that it is healing to the souls of those who listen to it, and it has the power to make them happy."*

Later in the year, Kenzaburo wrote and narrated a television program *Does the World Remember Hiroshima?* for NHK, Japan's equivalent of the BBC, in which he visited intellectuals in several countries, interviewing them about nuclear issues. It was broadcast in August, to commemorate the bombing. The producer was Yoshiaki Yamato, senior producer in the Current Affairs Program Division, who had been creating television programs both with and about Kenzaburo Oe for some fifteen years—thirteen programs in all. Mr. Yamato commissioned a piece from Hikari *(Hiroshima*

*The asterisk here, and throughout the chapter, follows translations by Anita Keire.

Requiem) for the soundtrack, where it is played and sung in various arrangements, and the program includes scenes of Kenzaburo explaining the commission to Hikari and discussing the piece with him.

This national exposure proved helpful to Mr. Okano in getting approval for the production of Hikari's CD; recording sessions were scheduled on June 8 and 9, 1992, a few days before Hikari's twenty-ninth birthday, in Nippon Columbia's studio in Tokyo. The instrumentalists would be Ms. Ebi and, playing the flute, Hiroshi Koizumi, an eminent musician, best known as a pioneer of contemporary-classical repertory, who had become a friend of the Oes through Toru Takemitsu. Hikari was pleased but could not understand the implications of the project. Before the session, he told a reporter from the *Mainichi,* a major Tokyo daily, that he was happy about the CD, "but I don't make any money so I might not be able to buy it."‡

For the first recording session, Hikari came with his mother and father. He apparently found their trip by subway, and their search for the studio in an unfamiliar neighborhood, quite exhausting. Unwell by the time they reached the building, he had a seizure in the elevator and had to lie down for a while on folding chairs his parents lined up for him; they also wrung out towels and held them to his forehead. He recovered well enough to participate in the recording session, giving precise answers to the pianist's questions about emphasis and tempo, though according to his father's account he was rather subdued. A newspaper reporter came to cover the session and attempted to interview Hikari, but the composer only cocked his head and listened to the questions without replying. In an essay in *A Healing Family,* Kenzaburo described the contrast between this failed attempt at communication and the complete communication Hikari achieved with the musicians that day.

Mr. Okano said, "The only piece that was a problem was 'Graduation,' which was the first composition in the first collection

‡The double dagger here, and throughout the chapter, follows translations by Martha Serrille.

of scores produced at the Oes' expense. Although it is a short piece with a very beautiful melody, it does not stand up as a piano solo, . . . although it would be O.K. as a song, since there are three verses. . . . I suddenly came up with the idea that it could be rewritten as variations for the flute, with this melody as the theme. When I made the suggestion, Hikari said, 'Well . . . ' The next thing I knew, he started to draw lines on a score sheet. I was able to see clearly music being born from Hikari's head."*

Mr. Okano felt completely satisfied with Hikari's revised version of "Graduation," which was the last piece to be recorded, on the second day. "A slight tension could be felt running through the performers and the others who were present. *Take one.* An introduction in a D-minor chord begins with broken chords on the piano. Then the theme in eight measures on the flute. Variation section with all of four variations. Minor chords to major chords. From andante to adagio, then allegro. It is short, but resplendent, and full of tension as the theme returns after passing through a variety of scenarios. The resulting theme is played with an obviously highly charged emotion, compared to the first time it appears. Then there's a coda which seems to disappear into thin air. Even when the last sound had completely disappeared after the tape had ended, no one uttered a word," he said.*

A few days after the recording was made, the Oes left for Kenzaburo's home village in Shikoku; for several years, Kenzaburo had celebrated Hikari's birthday by bringing musicians there to give concerts that included his music. "Hikari's music is something everyone can understand. The people in my village criticize my novels, say they can't understand them, but they appreciate Hikari's music. The only times the villagers welcomed me was when I invited musicians to give these concerts there, playing the works of my Hikari along with Beethoven, Chopin, and Schubert. They made a big sensation in my village; six hundred people would come—that's half the population."

The disc was released four months later. To coincide with the release, a concert, introduced with a lecture by Kenzaburo, was given on October 29 in Tokyo. During the rehearsal, Hikari, worried about the success of the performance, had a mild seizure. He recovered fully in time for the concert, though, which was a triumph, sold out and respectfully reviewed in important newspapers. But like most of Hikari's press coverage, the reviews and articles about the event focused as much on Kenzaburo and on his unusual relationship with his son as on the music itself.

"I was very anxious for Mr. Okano at that time," Kenzaburo remembers. "He was a young man, taking a chance with his career on my son's work. What if the CD was a flop? He had said that a disc would have to sell 2000 copies not to be considered a failure, so I was determined to buy 2000 copies myself, so that he wouldn't suffer from the risk he was taking for my son. But I had no idea how I was going to come up with the money for 2000 CDs. But on the same day he told me that figure, I got a phone call from NHK, asking me to do a half-year series of lectures about literature. I asked how much they would pay me, and it was exactly the amount I would need to buy the 2000 CDs. So I agreed, and lectured on television for six months. The first run of the CDs was 600 copies, and I bought 300 of them right away, intending to buy the other 300 as soon as NHK had paid me for the lectures; I phoned Mr. Okano the following week to tell him I had the money for the rest. But he said there were no more copies—the CDs had already sold out. After that, they produced more, and it was literally like wildfire. And this was with no advertising at all, only word of mouth."

In Japan's classical-music recording industry, sales of 10,000 are considered a smash success. *The Music of Hikari Oe* sold 80,000 within three months of its release—Nippon Columbia's best-seller ever by far in the classical-music category and the top seller in classical music recordings in Japan that year. It won the Grand Prix Gold Disc, Japan's top classical-music award. Obviously, Kenzaburo Oe's fame and his readers' curiosity about the disabled son he had been writing about for so many years was responsible to some extent for the runaway sales. But to what extent? The first CD of Hikari's music came out two years before Kenzaburo won the Nobel prize, at a time when his career was not flourishing notably. He estimates that he has forty or fifty thousand loyal readers in Japan, no more.

So the quality of the music had something to do with it— along, no doubt, with curiosity about a mentally handicapped composer. Mr. Okano said, "Hikari's music is very fresh. Before Hikari, most classical CDs were geared toward commercialism or the scholarly extreme. But Hikari created a new music approachable by a broader audience."

All the journalists who have written about Hikari, both here and in Japan, have stressed the discrepancy between his musical achievements and his cognitive limitations. In Japan, the nearest thing to a conventional record review ran in *Sports Nippon* on October 4, 1992, in Kyoku Miyajima's classical-music column under the headline A Collection of Hikari Oe's Compositions to Be Released October 21st / Clarity Reminiscent of Mozart:

> Twenty-five short pieces have been gathered together for this CD. Although all of them are reminiscent of practice pieces, every melody flows extremely naturally because it does not feel as though there are artificial sections for any of the pieces at all. The overall sound also has the clarity of polished crystal. It would not even be an exaggeration to say that this clarity is like that in the compositions of Mozart, the child prodigy. It would be fair to say that the indescribable feeling of "gentleness" in all of the pieces is characteristic of Hikari's compositions. If you listened to this CD when you felt tired, from work or your life, I think that the tension in your shoulders would quietly slip away, and the fatigue that had been weighing down heavily upon you would suddenly disappear completely.*

Generally, the stories that appeared about Hikari in the Japanese press in 1992, while tending to assume that readers would be familiar with his disabilities from his father's writings about him, told how Hikari's music came to be written rather than describing the music itself. The news, in those stories, was that this well-known member of Kenzaburo Oe's family had, despite the disabilities that would seem to preclude it, become a composer, and that a CD of his work was about to be released or, depending on the date of the stories, had been released, and was selling in extraordinary numbers.

Many of the stories include serious thoughts from Kenzaburo: "I had been the one trying all the time to heal Hikari, but when . . . I heard my son's music for the first time . . . I felt myself healing.‡ (*Yomiuri Shimbun,* one of the major Tokyo dailies, October 5, 1992.) Or, "What does it mean to be handicapped? It means that there is a wall between you and other people. However, through the performance [of my son's music], that wall is cleared away. Hikari's inner world has found an avenue of expression that does not require our intervention."* (*Tokyo News,* October 23, 1992.) Some included interviews with Hikari's mother, his piano teacher, the instrumentalists who recorded the CD, or Hiroyuki Okano: "Hikari is fun to be with and a very appealing guy. His music is unadulterated, too."‡ (*Tokyo Shimbun,* October 4, 1992.)

In November, one business-focused paper published an essay from a former teacher of handicapped children, now handicapped himself, reflecting on how and why Hikari's music moved him. "Hikari Oe has done me the favor of giving me, as I am now, that much more courage. Thank you, Hikari," he wrote.* In December, a sports-paper columnist wrote about his own failed attempts at composing; he said that Hikari's success caused him "to appreciate the greatness of composers and the limits of amateurs all over again."* No doubt the kind of publicity Hikari received, especially the personal nature of the responses of many of those who were writing about him, attracted an unusually broad range of listeners to his music.

A long, detailed feature in a culturally oriented weekly, *Shukan Shincho,* titled "The People Who Discovered the Musical Talents of Hikari Oe, the Handicapped Person Currently in the Spotlight," posed the question, "Is 'The Music of Hikari Oe' a classic?," concluding that Hikari had created music that must be recognized as extraordinary, even apart from its astonishing popularity. The article also included Kenzaburo's thoughts on Hikari's unexpected success: "Our family life would not have amounted to much without music. That includes my writing, too! We have been able to get on with our lives because of music. Without it, I think one of us—either my wife or I—would have given up. So the most frightening thing I can think of is what would have happened if there had been no music in our lives.

"Nevertheless, we never expected that our Pooh-chan's compositions would be made into a recording or anything like that. Not even a little. So of course we never thought that they would be performed in a real concert. When a young man from a record company came to visit, I did idly imagine how thrilled I would be if a record were to be made. But I never dreamed it would enjoy this kind of reception. I don't think this will be a turning point in Hikari's life, or that this is the beginning of a career as a composer for him. I think of these events as a kind of fabulous festival that has happened in our house. Besides, Hikari himself has more or less forgotten about it, and is returning to a quiet life.

"Still, I feel that I have in a way been released from this child of mine when I can see this recording of something called 'his music' right before my eyes. He hasn't been thinking of what has happened as an opportunity, but I—as the father who has written stories about him—think I must use it to move in a different direction as a writer."*

Hikari was, of course, delighted at his sudden success. Soon after the release, he received more than one hundred fan letters. He kept them in a box near his bed and reread them from time to time.

The following spring, an old friend of the family invited the Oes to take Hikari to Europe for a mostly musical holiday. His parents worried about his fitness for a long plane trip and about how he would adjust to living in hotels for three weeks. In fact, the trip went very well. They left on June 9, when all Japan was thoroughly mesmerized by Crown Prince Naruhito's wedding, and Hikari celebrated his thirtieth birthday in Salzburg.

One of the high points of the Oes' itinerary was a night at the Vienna Staatsoper. Kenzaburo had wondered whether Hikari would be able to sit through five hours of Wagner. This, after all, is a young man who does not watch movies because he cannot follow the plots, and the plot of the Ring cycle is so notoriously complicated that it has given rise to a virtual subgenre of classical-music humor. *Siegfried* held him spellbound, though: "he listened, rapt, almost as if breathing it in." Did he understand the plot? His father doesn't think so. But Hikari had *lived* some of Siegfried's story, for all the world like a character in a Kenzaburo Oe novel who finds himself enacting a legend from folklore in real life. Just like Siegfried, he began by understanding birdsong.

In Chur, where the Oes stayed before boarding the train for Salzburg, Hikari was absorbed in listening to the calls of various birds in the courtyard of their hotel. His father questioned him about whether their songs were like those of the Japanese birds on the record that first inspired Hikari to speak. Asked if one was like a Japanese robin, Hikari smiled and said, "Only the pitch is different!"

Kenzaburo Oe wrote an essay about the trip called "Seiji Ozawa's Chair." He discussed the family's visit to Salzburg, including an account of Hikari's delight in recognizing the conductor's name on a nameplate on a chair in the Kobenzl Hotel, where the Oes were staying, a hotel where many classical musicians stay during the summer music festival.

The trip prompted him to reflect on how the unity of his family is preserved although father, mother, and son have different interests. On their train trip to Salzburg, he himself reflected on the travel diaries he remembered from his days as a student of French literature; Hikari was "listening to the scenery," which was, of course, very exotic to him, and Yukari pressed her face to the window when the train passed meadows where interesting wildflowers could be seen.

On the way back to Japan, the family stopped over briefly in Paris, for the odd reason that Kenzaburo had an interest in the remains of some French royalty, including Henri IV and Catherine de Médicis, who had been buried in the cathedral of St. Denis and exhumed during the French Revolution—an interest awakened by an essay on the subject by Kazuo Watanabe, the authority on Rabelais who had been his mentor when he was a student of French literature. Kenzaburo wanted to be in Paris in case he could learn something from any events that might be scheduled to commemorate the two hundredth anniversary of the vandalizing of these graves.

As it happened, there was an arts festival at St. Denis just then; Mr. Ozawa was conducting Mahler's Third Symphony, and the Oes were able to get tickets. Kenzaburo had concluded after first meeting Ozawa that he was "one of the best people of his age I'd ever met." Seeing him in France more than three decades later, he reflected on how the cosmopolitan nature of his success—dramatically exemplified by his leading a French orchestra and chorus with an American soloist in German music—had added to his impressiveness. And Hikari was plainly impressed too, proudly reminding his parents during the intermission that he had eaten dinner in Seiji Ozawa's special chair in the hotel in Salzburg.

Hikari spent his thirtieth birthday in that hotel. The owner, noticing a fax someone had sent with a drawing of a birthday cake on it, gave Hikari a present, and the Oes reciprocated by giving her one of Hikari's CDs. After listening to it several times, she told the Oes the next day that she felt Hikari's music reflected the benefits of his having been raised in such a positive way by his parents, and that she believed her own family happiness had a similar cause.

Hikari seemed fascinated by everything musical he encountered on the trip—not just the live performances but visits to museums to see Mozart and Beethoven scores, and a trip to the church where "Silent Night" is said to have been composed. He spent most of his evenings composing in hotel rooms. Later, wondering how his son really felt on that vacation, Kenzaburo looked at snapshots and noticed that Hikari's expression was emotionless except when he was involved in something musical. Kenzaburo decided that music gives Hikari a sense of being at home, just as writing fiction gives Kenzaburo himself this sense, wherever he happens to be.

Just six months after his happy, music-centered European holiday, Hikari's health took a sharp turn for the worse, and it looked for a while as if his extraordinary composing career might be short-lived. He had many seizures during the early months of 1994, sometimes as many as four in a single day. For the first time since his teens, he lost interest in composing. His mother said, "They were the worst fits he had experienced since he was born. I thought that his creative work might be impossible after that." Hikari rallied, though, celebrating his return to health by composing a piece called "Salzburg," slightly over one minute long, which had been inspired by the visit to Mozart's birthplace.

Throughout all this, he was still Japan's best-selling composer in the classical-music category. In the seven months since its release, *Music of Hikari Oe* had been holding its place at the top of the classical-music charts. Its rocket-blast soar to the highest spot, with no promotion, was amazing enough, but the fact that it could stay there so long with no advertising whatsoever is even more amazing. It continued to sell at the astonishing rate of nearly five hundred copies a day, setting a record that would not be surpassed until the release of Hikari's second CD.

Turning Points

Before the end of that eventful year, the possibility of "a quiet life" was over for Hikari. And for Kenzaburo, who had known so little peace since beginning his writing career, even quiet moments would become increasingly unobtainable. Hikari had become well known through his father's fiction and then famous in his own right because of the unprecedented success of his first CD. By the time his second CD was recorded, on June 27, 28, and 29, 1994, not long after his thirty-first birthday, a crew from NHK was on hand to film the event for another documentary of Mr. Yamato's, this one about Hikari and Kenzaburo's relationship. The program is structured around events in that summer, with forays into the past explaining Kenzaburo and Hikari's previous histories. Mr. Yamato said that in the course of working with Kenzaburo over so many years, he had developed a very special feeling for Hikari, and the programs he created about him, especially this one, gave Hikari the stature of a supercelebrity, recognized and hailed by strangers on the street wherever he went in Japan.

Kenzaburo has described how seriously Hikari took the news of this impending television appearance. Typically, he saw it as entailing responsibilities. His father explained to him that he would be interviewed on camera; to practice for this, he spoke into a tape-recorder microphone at home, taking great care with his speech. The improvement was dramatic after only a week of practice; it was noticeable at once to one of his doctors, who had called on the phone to arrange an appointment.

To achieve optimum sound, the CD sessions were done in studios in Asahikawa City Taisetsu Crystal Hall on Hokkaido, Japan's northernmost island; this trip was truly exhausting for Hikari, who came with his mother. During one of them, he had a seizure, which was filmed by the television crew and included in the broadcast.

This is not the only troubling segment in the documentary. It begins with Kenzaburo and Hikari discussing a request they have received from a group of disabled people in Hiroshima; they want to present a concert of Hikari's music there, and Kenzaburo suggests a new piano-and-flute piece for the occasion, which Hikari does go on to write. Parts of it are included in the segment of the program that covers the concert. Kenzaburo, whose involvement with antinuclear causes had begun with the trip he made to Hiroshima after Hikari's birth, had been unwilling to share his concerns with Hikari in the past. He expressed his reservations in a story he wrote in 1984 called "We Won't Go to Hiroshima." The father of a character based on Hikari rejects the idea of taking his son to the Peace Memorial Museum, because seizures have made the son particularly fearful of death, and his father feels that seeing the museum's horrifying displays would only upset him: "That's a wound he'd never let even his father heal."

"Back then," Kenzaburo remembers, "I took the position that my son couldn't understand the tragedy of Hiroshima. So I wouldn't take him there. But now, Hikari is grown up. He's over thirty, and he's creating music. What with the progress he's made, we seem to be able to understand together the pictures and stories about Hiroshima. I want to pass all this on to him if I can."

And they did visit the museum together. On camera, Kenzaburo showed Hikari the section of the bomb-damaged hospital wall displayed there. "The blast blew glass into it, and made it all rough," he explained. Then they went upstairs, to the part of the museum that shows recreated scenes of the city just after the bomb fell.

Hikari was plainly frightened and distressed. In the television footage, he looks utterly miserable, standing still, refusing to go on, grinding his fist under his ear and against his throat. His father tells him, "Come on, it's O.K. Are you scared? You don't have to be scared. Come on. You O.K.?" Gently, he puts his hand on Hikari's back, simultaneously comforting him and urging him ahead.

Kenzaburo had expected Hikari to be upset but felt he had become strong enough to withstand such a distressing experience, and that the emotions it engendered might eventually be used in a constructive way. When he asked what Hikari thought of the museum, Hikari was so wretched that his answer came out in garbled form: "It's was all awful."

"I see," Kenzaburo said. "You thought it was no good. But you won't forget." Hikari nodded. "Not forgetting is good. It's really a great thing, not to forget," Kenzaburo told him.

Hikari's reaction later inspired Kenzaburo to write an essay about the healing power of artistic creation. The piece is essentially his answer to those who have accused him of exploiting his son. Noting that he replayed the scene from a videotape several times, Kenzaburo observes, apropos the garbled sentence, that Hikari never allows himself to speak sloppily. He "seemed terrified, more so than I had ever seen him before," his father writes. Yet he feels there must have been something deliberate in his choice of words and speculates that his son's use of the present tense might imply some condemnation of himself, for having forced him to view such horrifying things.

He then discusses an anonymous attack, written with a word processor and printed on an announcement for a concert in celebration of the release of Hikari's second CD. It had been left in the mud next to the Oes' mailbox, leading them to wonder whether the author could be one of their neighbors: after all, who would go out of their way to deliver it personally to Setagaya when they might have sent it in the mail? The note said that Hikari's music would not have been performed or recorded if he were not the son of a celebrity, and adds that many talented composers can't get their work performed, concluding "I'd like you to know what most experts really think of your son's music!"

Kenzaburo's response was embodied in the lecture he wrote to introduce his son's music at the concert in question. It begins by saying that the music the audience is about to hear was written by someone who has never cried, and—although one of the pieces is called "Dream"—may never have had a dream. (No amount of persistent questioning by his parents has been able to clarify that question.) Describing Hikari's musical voice as that of "a wailing soul," Kenzaburo noted how his music had deepened since his earlier, cheerier compositions.

He points out that Hikari's verbal abilities are limited, but that he has extraordinary powers of musical concentration. Invoking the philosopher Simone Weil's definition of prayer as a special kind of concentration, a "directing of all the attention of which the soul is capable," he examines the spiritual aspects of artistic creation, citing another passage in Weil's writing. She discusses a legend about the Holy Grail, in which a knight who was seeking it asked the wounded king who guarded it, "In what way are you suffering?" His question proves him the worthy successor as guardian of the Grail. Kenzaburo says that is the question everyone has asked who has helped Hikari, that it is the question the audience members must be asking at the concert, and that it is the question his music answers.

Kenzaburo concludes by explaining that (presumably because of the attack) he had departed from his previous policy of escorting Hikari—who needs help because of his problems with motion and vision—to the stage to take bows after concerts, sending Yukari instead. Watching them together there after the concert where he delivered the lecture, he felt he was seeing a scene from their lives after his own death. But while writing literally about his own death, he appears to have also had a kind of metaphorical death unconsciously in mind—a renunciation of his creative life.

The television documentary includes shots of Kenzaburo finishing his mammoth trilogy, *The Blazing Green Tree,* actually writing its last word, which is (in English) "Rejoyce! [*sic*]" He says it is "the end of the line" for him. Hikari made a sort of cameo appearance—as himself—in that trilogy. "The main character visits the house of someone I called K—that is, Kenzaburo Oe—and is talking with the Oe family. One of the main characters is a young man who became famous as a composer of popular music. But he left that field, and has come to Japan to study the folklore, legends, and indigenous religions of the Japanese people. On his visit to my house, he spoke about his music with Hikari, and Hikari could read his scores, so they talked—and that's all, that's the only role Hikari plays in that work," Kenzaburo says.

Six days after the release of Hikari's second CD and two days before the documentary was broadcast, Kenzaburo made a startling announcement, amplifying what he had said on camera about having reached the "end of the line": he had decided to give up writing fiction because of Hikari's success. He said that for years, his primary motivation in writing had been to give Hikari a voice. Now that Hikari was established as a composer, with a voice of his own, Kenzaburo felt no further need to create a means of expression for him. He told a reporter from the *Asahi* (yet another major Tokyo daily), "We wanted our son, who does not speak, to relate what was in his heart at least a little. I could never even have tried to imagine that Hikari could express his feelings to the extent that he has. I feel that his problems are heading toward resolution, not just in terms of my stories, but in real life. I do not intend to give up being a man of letters; I will continue to write essays, etc."*

The documentary aired as a "Special," in prime time on September 18, 1994, the day after the news of Kenzaburo's announcement was published. It shaped Hikari's image for an audience of millions in his country. It was for the most part warmly received, though some critics felt that showing Hikari's seizure was in poor taste and objected to the shots of the handicapped who welcomed Hikari to Hiroshima. Most viewers responded enthusiastically, though, and the year after it was aired in Japan, the program was sent to several foreign countries after winning an International Emmy.

By September 28, in an article about Kenzaburo's surprising decision, the *People*-like weekly *SPA* reported that the combined sales of Hikari's two CD's had reached 100,000. The piece included an interview with Kenzaburo, who explained his renunciation:

> It's not that I'm giving up writing. The final part of *The Blazing Green Tree* will be published next spring, and . . . after that, I have no plans. To come up with a new novel and new subject matter, starting from scratch, might take me another ten years. That would make me seventy, but of course I'll be dead by then.

*The asterisk here, and throughout the chapter, follows translations by Anita Keire.

Characterizing Hikari as "one of the most popular artists of today," whose "concerts are routinely sold out," the article quoted Kenzaburo on his son's success:

> I don't think of it as true independence, because he still can't live by himself. And yet he is able to communicate with other people through something that he has created himself, through the CDs. My son, who cannot participate in normal social activity, who has lived all his life within the protection of his family, is having all kinds of communication with other people, without our intervention. This gives me the greatest joy. I always had a feeling inside that drove me to try to express things for Hikari, on his behalf. But I don't have to do that anymore. I'd like to spend some time reading Spinoza—I've been saving him up. Hikari can support me for a while.

A photograph of Kenzaburo and Hikari is captioned, "The son takes over from the father, who will start a new life as a *retired* novelist. The changing of the guard for the Oe family brings us a new generation in creative expression."‡

By October 3, Hikari's second CD was in the number-one spot on the classical charts, and the first CD was number four; the double placement set yet another record for a living composer in the classical category. Rejoicing in his son's success, Kenzaburo was looking forward to spending the rest of his life in tranquil retirement. In fact, the tranquillity lasted for just ten days.

The announcement that Kenzaburo had won the Nobel Prize in literature was made on October 13. The news came to the Oes over the phone; Hikari answered, but, because the caller was speaking English, handed the receiver to his mother. Hikari takes his phone-answering responsibilities seriously, and found the ceaseless round of calls that followed the announcement quite exhausting. Sakurao told a reporter that his brother "looked a little tired" by the end of the day.‡

‡The double dagger here, and throughout the chapter, follows translations by Martha Serrille.

Media coverage of Kenzaburo's award stressed the role Hikari had played in his father's work, including accounts of his career as a composer and often mentioning the NHK documentary. The *Mainichi* said,

> The strength of Mr. Oe's love for his son Hikari, obvious even at first glance, is almost painful to witness. When he is writing his fiction, Mr. Oe gently addresses his son, Hikari, near at hand as he writes notes on a score sheet while lying on the floor, or turns toward the piano. Mr. Oe says that he has learned something tremendous from Hikari's compositions. "Hikari, who does not express himself in words, has been able to avail himself of his music to develop. Through this," Mr. Oe says, "he taught me that the act of expressing yourself is healing to the heart." Hikari's coming into his own in this way as a musician may provide a kind of resolution for Mr. Oe's literature, which has taken as one theme the question of how to live with a child who is mentally handicapped. "From a certain point on, the task of expressing in his stead that which Hikari could not express in words was my work, but it seems to me that he is communicating in his own unique way with people at large through music without my intercession, so I feel that it is meddlesome of me to stand in the middle," says Mr. Oe.*

The article emphasizes Hikari's importance in his father's story in a striking way, concluding with the words of Shizue Itoh, the director of Hikari's vocational center: "You can see it when they drop off or pick up Hikari; they take Hikari in, and the family really seems like a harmonious family of equals. I really think it's doubly joyous that Hikari has turned thirty and established himself in the musical field."*

Takashi Tachibana may have hit upon the rationale that prompted Kenzaburo's renunciatory impulse. In the course of an hour-long televised conversation with Kenzaburo after the Nobel announcement, Mr. Tachibana said, speaking of Hikari's music, "The real Hikari—the Hikari who creates this music—is greater than the Hikari you imagined, and created in your writing." Reporters asked Kenzaburo whether the prize would make him reconsider his renunciation of fiction; he insisted his decision was final.

He reaffirmed that his decision had been based on the fact that Hikari had "found a real resolution . . . in real life, not just in my stories."‡ Recognition of Hikari's work meant far more to him than the glorification of his own: "The outside world is able to understand something of the inner life of my child, in spite of his intellectual handicap. This to me is a much greater event than my winning the Nobel Prize."‡

Immediately after the prize announcement, the Japanese government offered Kenzaburo the Order of Culture, the highest honor Japan can bestow for achievement in the arts and humanities. Because the award is given through the Emperor, Kenzaburo, who has bitterly opposed the emperor system during his entire adult life, mocking it in his literature and blaming it for everything he finds deplorable in Japanese history, culture, and society, refused the honor. He now explains his refusal as an expression of his disapproval of the government acting through the Emperor in such ways. This was a truly outrageous gesture in Japan—far more shocking than, say, declining a knighthood or an O.B.E. would be in Great Britain and all the more shocking when made by a figure who had just brought his country glory by winning the world's most prestigious literary award. After all, it's only five decades since the Emperor was officially a god, and there's no equivalent at all in Japan for the substantial, perennial opposition to the monarchy in England. His refusal shocked many people deeply. Conservatives were, predictably, enraged, but even moderates were alienated. People who had found his rebelliousness endearing or refreshing in the past thought he had gone too far, seeing the gesture as gratuitously ungracious, even downright bratty. It kept Kenzaburo's name in the news, prolonging the public scrutiny that followed the Nobel award and changing its nature: the publicity was entirely negative now.

Kenzaburo made this alienated and alienating gesture at a moment when the Japanese public's reception of Hikari's work was enthusiastic enough to be called a craze. An odd article in a Tokyo sports paper reported Kenzaburo's spurning the order and also featured an interview about Hikari's CDs with a Kyoto record-store owner, Eiji Shimizu, noting that nationwide sales of both discs together had reached 120,000 (500 in Mr. Shimizu's store alone). "Although the store played Hikari's discs to promote them, Mr. Shimizu said that most of the customers who had flocked to buy the CDs had heard about Hikari's music by word of mouth. He said about half of them were sufferers from insomnia who had heard that there was something peculiarly relaxing about the music. Mr. Shimizu speculated that the simplicity of Hikari's music might generate the kind of alpha waves in the brain that characterize a relaxed state. 'I think they probably reduce stress,' he said."*

Up to this point, most of the media attention father and son had received had been friendly. Now, dissenting voices broke in. One magazine ran a survey on the subject "Does Oe Flaunt His Disabled Son Too Much?" (Most of the answers were ambiguous; some pointed out that the media, not Kenzaburo, were doing the flaunting.) The composer Ryuichi Sakamoto published an essay in the January 1995 issue of the arts magazine *Eureka,* condemning Hikari's music as a kind of "victim art." "There should be a line between the artistic merit of music and the issue of the handicapped. Should all the music created by the handicapped be given credit?" he wrote. But Hikari's spectacular sales were unaffected by such attacks: *Music of Hikari Oe 2* occupied the number-one spot on classical-category sales charts, and the first CD, *Music of Hikari Oe,* remained in the top thirty.

By the end of January 1995, Hikari had been shown on news programs all over the world, and there can scarcely have been anyone in Japan who had not seen him on TV at least once. He accompanied Kenzaburo when he went to Stockholm to receive the

Nobel Prize and deliver his acceptance speech. Mr. Yamato made yet another documentary about Kenzaburo and Hikari; coverage of the events related to the Nobel award was interspersed with Hikari's activities in Sweden. He was shown composing a piece called "Ocean" in the Oes' hotel suite in Stockholm. Akiko Ebi flew in from Paris to visit the family there and played the piece on camera under Hikari's direction; back in the suite, Kenzaburo learned what Hikari's new work sounded like through a videotape of her performance. The documentary included footage of Hikari disco dancing at a Swedish institute for the handicapped that stresses music therapy; some Japanese critics found the sequence distasteful.

By the time Sakamoto's attack was published, one in every two hundred households in Japan owned one of Hikari's CDs, a fact that is all the more remarkable considering that only half of Japan's population owned CD players then. Surely many listeners wanted to like Hikari's music because of the personal triumph it represented. But the continuing success of his CDs suggests that listeners were motivated to buy them in such extraordinary numbers for reasons that went beyond curiosity, sympathy, or following a fad. There can be no doubt that his appealing, accessible music brought his audience real pleasure and enjoyment.

The Oes have been attacked for exploiting Hikari, but they have actually shown great restraint in their involvement with the way his music is marketed. They have repeatedly turned down requests for concerts and promotional activities that they feel are purely commercial, and they give Hikari's health and well-being top priority in scheduling his activities. They say it has also been charged that Hikari's success would have been impossible without the fame he had attained through his father's works. There may be a little truth in this, but the sales history of Hikari's CDs in America, where his father, even after the Nobel award, could scarcely be called a celebrity, suggests something else.

And in fact Hikari's sales in Japan could not have depended

entirely on Kenzaburo's celebrity status. Hikari's initial success occurred at a time when Kenzaburo was no more in the news than usual. If the staggering commercial success of the first CD had been a result simply of Kenzaburo's fame as such, the broadcast of the NHK program right after the release of the second should have resulted in something like doubled sales, especially because the Nobel award was announced almost immediately afterward. *Music of Hikari Oe 2* was indeed a record-breaking blockbuster in the classical category, selling 100,000 copies in the three months after its release. Yet its sales didn't outdo the first CD's (80,000 in the first three months) by the dramatic margin that might have been expected, especially when the two subsequent waves of publicity about Hikari (the one that followed Kenzaburo's surprising announcement and the one that followed the Nobel award) are taken into consideration. The Nobel Prize sent Kenzaburo's own sales skyrocketing—over 1 million copies of his works were sold in Japan that year.

In America, Kenzaburo had received no more publicity than any other literary Nobel laureate from a faraway country, and his spurning the Order of Culture was, naturally, barely noticed. Both of Hikari's CDs were released simultaneously in this country in January 1995 on the Denon label, and with scarcely any publicity of any kind—some brief coverage in a daytime show on National Public Radio and a few inconspicuous reviews—they sold out entirely in their first week in the stores. So media attention appears to have been entirely irrelevant to his initial success here, but it's impossible to know how many American purchases were prompted by curiosity stimulated by learning about such an unusual composer at the time his father won the Nobel Prize and how many were driven by exposure to his work itself. More extensive press coverage followed gradually, peaking in the spring, and an NBC *Nightline* program was aired in December.

Hikari's music has continued to sell itself. French and German releases followed the American. As of April 1997, both CDs together had sold a staggering 300,000 copies worldwide. Kenzaburo says that's $8 million worth of recordings. When asked if he was perfectly sure of that astonishing figure, he said drily, "I'm the one who reads his royalty statements—I ought to know," and added with characteristic delight in being somehow outdone by Hikari, "That's five times more than my books have made." Even after the Nobel Prize? "The sales because of the prize are still going on, of course," (in the spring of 1997) "but so far—yes," he said.

Hikari was once asked by an interviewer how long he intended to go on composing. He turned to his father and asked, "How many pieces of music paper do we have left?" Fame and fortune have given Hikari a new sense of himself. In his own right, he has become as much of a celebrity as his illustrious father and his glamorous uncle Juzo Itami. Strangers recognize and hail him whenever he goes out. Kenzaburo says that Hikari doesn't understand the financial aspects of his spectacular career at all, but he knows he is an artist, a successful one—and that many people enjoy his music. He cherishes their fan letters and treasures his relationships with the musicians he has come to know through his work. Recently, one of his teachers at Karasuyama inquired whether music was his hobby. "Listening to music is my hobby," he replied, "but making it is my job."

"The Subject of Great Amazement"

What does Hikari's music sound like? And how good is it, really? As Hikari's press coverage shows, it is barely possible to describe— never mind evaluate—his work without taking his circumstances into account. A wide variety of listeners inside and outside the musical community have described and evaluated his music, and their feelings about him have inevitably affected their responses: some were dismissive, some passionately moved. In an article that came out two months after the release of the second CD, the popular Japanese poet and literary critic Makoto Ooka said, "It would probably be more accurate to say that it is the subject of great amazement than to say that it is greatly praised."*

Kenzaburo's characterizations of Hikari's music have, understandably, always been colored by his overwhelming emotional involvement with his son. In his liner notes for the second CD, he describes some of the pieces as expressing "the voice of a soul wailing in darkness." He has often said that composing enabled Hikari to express feelings. For example, "Requiem for M," written in 1984 when Hikari's doctor, Nobuo Moriyasu, died of cancer, proved that Hikari was capable of feeling grief: he had had a severe seizure on learning of his physician's death and wrote the "Requiem" as soon as he recovered. And when he heard "Dream" for the first time, Kenzaburo said, "I'm simply amazed. I realized that my son was creating music, that it was taking shape, but this level is so much more than I ever expected. In the world of music, he can think, feel, create so freely. I don't even have the power to comment on his work. It's beyond me."

Yet Kenzaburo seems somewhat ambivalent about how Hikari's music should be judged. He assigns some irritation with extramusical assessments of Hikari's work to Ma-chan, the character inspired by his daughter, Natsumiko, in *A Quiet Life,* having her say,

> When Father published Eeyore's music, at his own expense, and distributed copies to his friends and acquaintances, not a few of them said that they heard in it a mystical voice that transcended the limitations of human beings. Such sentimental impressions, I thought, though as usual these were words I uttered only in my heart. Eeyore starts working on each piece after carefully deliberating what he wants to express in it, which is what he did even for

*The asterisk here, and throughout the chapter, follows translations by Anita Keire.

pieces like "Summer in Kita-Karuizawa" or "Requiem for M." He's accumulated his technique through years of listening to FM programs and records, along with Mrs. T's patient instruction. He can't comment on his music the way ordinary musicians so eloquently do about theirs, but I think he creates his music by employing the themes and syntax of the people who walk or have walked this earth, and not at the suggestion of any heavenly will.

Mr. Ooka's reminiscences about having heard Hikari's music at a reading from *M/T and the Marvels of the Forest* appear to be an example of the kind of thing Kenzaburo had in mind. Ooka wrote, "The purity of the sound of the melodies made it seem for a moment as if the theatre had become completely transparent and was made entirely of air. The best description of it is 'heavenly.' . . . When loving performances by well-known musicians breathe life into his melodies, the result is truly miraculous, not just because a brain-damaged man has achieved success in something, but because he is able to transform the heavenly elements hidden within our souls into sound that celebrates the happiness and sorrow of the human spirit. Here, there is not a fragment of evil. The music runs clear as a river that reflects the variety of the human spirit, the blue of the sky, the white of the cloud, and the black of the shadow. That is not to say there is no darkness in the music. It also contains the anxiety and trembling of a pure, virgin, adolescent soul, in an inexhaustible flow so direct as to pierce the heart."‡ He has written similar effusions about specific pieces: "'Requiem for M' is a sad piece created around the time Hikari's primary physician died. From beginning to end, it modestly sings of things like the trembling apprehension of slowly hunting down some monstrous thing, the breaking of your heart, and the effort of trying to bring the pieces of your heart back together in a different way after steadfastly withstanding its breaking. 'Lullaby for Keiko' is a mov-

‡The double dagger here, and throughout the chapter, follows translations by Martha Serrille.

ing piece with a particularly beautiful melody line that nonetheless can only be said to be the singing of sorrow itself."* But that is, of course, the way a poet might be expected to respond to moving music.

Yoshiaki Yamato said, "I truly believe that the success of Hikari's CDs has been a result of his talent, and that it has nothing to do with his father's fame." He is a television producer, not a music critic, though, and he went on to talk not about the music but about Hikari himself: "Hikari is an extraordinary person. Whenever I meet him, I feel a kind of pull from the power of his spirit or his soul."

Hiroyuki Okano has spoken of experiencing overwhelming emotions when he first heard Hikari's music. But he has also spoken of it in measured terms that seem reasonable from a commercial record producer, restricting himself to discussions of Hikari's working methods, for example, when making lofty comparisons: "Maybe Hikari is like Mozart, after all. Not that his abilities are of the same quality as Mozart's, and I certainly don't know Mozart—but I think Hikari's approach to music is similar to his."

But what does Hikari's music actually sound like? It isn't indescribable—at least, no more so than any music ultimately is. It is entirely accessible, which no doubt accounts in part for its popularity. But only in part. While the early pieces are appealing primarily for their simplicity, freshness, and charm, some of the later, darker ones are extremely moving, with haunting melodies and striking elegance and economy of development. As in some short poetic forms, like haiku, much of their power comes from their compression. His pieces are very short, most shorter than three minutes. They are simple and written almost entirely in eighteenth- and nineteenth-century styles, showing few traces of influences later than Brahms. Kenzaburo has said that music is not an alternative to language for Hikari, but the language of Western classical music—Baroque, Classical, Romantic—is the only mode of expression he has truly and thoroughly mastered, and he seems to experience it as something not subject to change through time. This immediacy gives his pieces a notable freshness and directness, and some of them have great emotional power. Now and again, effects are achieved through surprises—unexpected modulations or dynamic variations—that are subtly reminiscent of the shifts in tone and bold juxtapositions in Kenzaburo's fiction.

There are twenty-five pieces on the first CD, mostly simple and engaging, but some, such as "Pied Piper," have an unexpected quality of wistfulness. "Mister Prelude" is particularly charming, a romp in the manner of Bach; savoring its not-taking-itself-seriously title adds to the listener's enjoyment. Some, such as the "Waltz in A Minor," have notably haunting melodies, sounding like something Chopin might have written in a version simplified for piano students. Others, such as the Rondo, could almost have been composed by an authentic Baroque composer. "Requiem for M" is slow, uses broken chords, and has an affecting minor melody; it's more complicated and ambitious than the previous pieces and seems to express the deepest feelings. "Lullaby for Keiko," which, the liner notes explain, was also written for Mrs. Moriyasu, the widow of the doctor who had cared for Hikari ever since he was born, has an appealing gentleness and directness. The Siciliano has greater sophistication, combining snaky chromaticism with subtly dramatic dynamics and a truly haunting melody; it's one of several pieces on this disc that could have been written only by an adult. "Grief"—for piano alone—begins very simply, so that the exposure of deep feeling as it ends is all the more affecting for being a surprise. The "Sad Waltz" seems to luxuriate lightly in its sadness—really rather Viennese and another very adult piece, full of subtle surprises. The longest piece, the "Hiroshima Requiem," has dignified sadness and moving sincerity.

The twenty-two pieces on the second CD are, as a whole, strikingly richer than those on the first. The range of periods it evokes shows Hikari coming into his own as a natural postmodernist, making unself-conscious use of eclectic elements from the things he's enjoyed in his long experience of listening to his favorite composers from various eras. Some, such as "Snow," express subtle feelings, despite a surface simplicity. "Grief No. 3," for solo piano, is an elegant and stylized exploration of a sorrowful emotion, reminiscent of Chopin. "Dream," Hikari's first violin piece, is also full of feeling and by no means childish, with an elusive quality of resigned melancholy in even its lightest moments. The "Siciliano in E Minor" is extraordinarily effective, with an unforgettable minor melodic line given sometimes to the flute, sometimes to the piano. It has a paradoxical quality—a subdued assertiveness—and its course is never predictable. The Adagio in D Minor for flute and piano is stunning, too, and its development also is full of agreeable and moving surprises. The well-named "Wistful Adagio" is a tour de force of economy, and "Nocturnal Capriccio" is probably Hikari's most completely successful work. Its sad, sinuously chromatic main melody is impossible to forget, and the piece is richly varied and deeply moving. The Andante Cantabile for violin and piano is a miracle of grace, quite theatrical, yet full of subtleties. Finally, the August Capriccio for violin and piano (another concert crowd pleaser), with its lovely, lyrical, somewhat Mendelssohnian melody, dramatic modulations, confident progress through elaborate, Baroque-style developments, and bold cadenza, is one of his most impressive and richly varied works.

The arrestingly titled "May the Plane Not Fall" is a sprightly piano evocation of soaring aerial motion. Kenzaburo explained its name: "Hikari used to worry that if my wife and I traveled together in the same aircraft and met with an accident, he along with his brother and sister would be deprived of both parents at one stroke. For this reason, I would never travel with my wife in the same aircraft. However, it once happened that my wife and I had to travel together to Europe. We left Hikari at home with his brother and sister on that occasion. In a mood of considerable anxiety, Hikari prayed that we would arrive safely at our destination."

Musicians who have worked with Hikari invariably include

emotional responses to his situation when asked to speak about what he has composed. In a *Tokyo News* interview after the release of his first CD, Akiko Ebi (the pianist on both his discs) said that Kenzaburo had sent her Hikari's scores on an impulse in 1988. The effect on her was overwhelming:

> The collection of sixteen short piano pieces communicated a gentle warmth like nothing I had seen before; they were very different from those issued by most publishers. Opening the cover page, I found what are actually very simple notes lined up between the staves on a musical sheet. I ran through all sixteen pieces in a flash, playing just the melody line because I was so eager to discover what music he had been influenced by. My first impression was that they were really delightful pieces overall, though there were also occasional places where I found I was thinking, Wait a minute, that's kind of odd, isn't it?
>
> My performance schedule has had me dividing my time between Japan and Europe for a long time. After my first experience of his music, I found myself putting Hikari Oe's scores in my bag and taking them with me to whichever country I was headed for. For me, it served as a sort of oasis from the stressful life of a professional musician; it provided a place where my heart could go to play.
>
> More than a year and a half after I had first come to know Hikari's music, something happened to me. Late one night, when I was feeling depressed, I happened to think of those pieces of his, so I pulled them out and was following the score slowly and deliberately on the piano. For some reason, as I played, tears kept welling up in my eyes and would not stop. For a long time I continued to play with tears in my eyes. The emotion I felt at that time is something I have never forgotten. Those tears were for the sadness I experienced in Hikari's music, but they also came out because Hikari's music freed me to feel the sadness that was in my heart at the time. At the same time, his music also coaxed the tears out by soothing the pain I was feeling.

There is a sincerity in the purity of his music—though it is in fact simple—which gives the listener peace of mind. It seems to me that this is where the soul of Hikari's music lies.*

Hiroshi Koizumi, the flutist on both CDs, reported being struck by unexpected depth in Hikari's pieces. "When I saw the scores for the first time, I thought his melodies were simple and unsophisticated," Mr. Koizumi said recently. "But when I played the pieces, I found them just beautiful. After playing them many times, I discovered that the simple melodies encompass sorrow, joy, and a variety of other feelings. I came to find his music very deep." Interviewed in 1994 about the success of Hikari's second CD, he said, "The breadth and depth of his expression expanded dramatically. He doesn't engage in conversation, but his feelings come through in his music. I believe that when he realized that there were many people listening to his music, the result was a vast expansion of his world, taking him far beyond his family, and that this has had a positive influence on his music."

Ken Noda, the pianist at a concert of Hikari's music in New York City on November 15, 1996, had given up a flourishing soloist's career five years before to work as musical assistant to James Levine, the director of the Metropolitan Opera. "I've played every composer there is," he said, "and this music definitely has a very special quality. It reminds me of Mozart, who is my favorite composer. He doesn't give you too much information, doesn't overload you. There are very few notes, but it speaks between the notes. It has unbelievable depth. It's childlike—and I don't mean anything like 'childish,' but I'm talking about how children have a wisdom and knowing beyond what you see. What touched me so deeply about Hikari is that he speaks a language we all know when we're young. It gets mucked up by the time we are adults. There can be an advantage to being unable to express yourself in a sophisticated way. Sometimes you can get to the truth because your mind isn't cluttered by too much education.

"And it's universal. Like his father's work, which I've read most of—Kenzaburo Oe's work breaks through boundaries and transcends categories, so I can't think of him as a Japanese writer, in the sense of being apart from the Western tradition. The word 'accessible' can have patronizing connotations, but Hikari Oe's music is accessible in the best sense. I do think, though, that there is a very Japanese melancholy in some of it. I'm looking forward to playing it. I realized when I first heard it that its simplicity provides exciting opportunities for imaginative interpretation."

He finds the "Hiroshima Requiem" particularly moving. "I'm a Japanese-American. I didn't even know about the Hiroshima bomb until I was sixteen. I grew up in a safe community in upstate New York. It wasn't until I went to Hiroshima that I realized what had happened to my people—took me rather late. I think Hikari Oe's Requiem expresses what he must have felt when he had the same realization. It captures exactly the grief and shock I felt at that late age," he said.

Cho-Liang Lin, the violinist at the same concert, has played a wide range of classical repertory under such eminent conductors as Charles Dutoit and Raymond Leppard, and has known and worked with Mr. Noda since they were students at Juilliard together (where Mr. Lin teaches now). He described Hikari's music as "very simple and charming, with pleasant and endearing harmonies. To me, it sounds a bit like Mozart mixed with Bach. It's very miniature and very classical. I read *A Personal Matter* and was very moved by it, and when I heard this music, it moved me, too. The appealing harmonies and straightforward forms should please everybody, even if they don't know anything about the composer's background."

Composers have spoken about his music, too, but their reactions were not unanimously appreciative. The Japanese composer Toshi Ichiyanagi has praised it, saying, "His music is so indescribably natural and easy, with its charmingly supported harmonic progressions and transitions." The Chinese composer Bright

Sheng, though, who had become curious about Hikari's music after reading about him and borrowed the CDs from a friend, said, "After finding out about him, I wanted to like the music. But to tell you the truth, I found it disappointing—thin, really. I didn't think there was much there." But another composer, Milos Raicovich, a Serbian who, like Hikari, writes in Classical style (a CD of his work is called "New Classicism"), had a completely different opinion. "I discovered Hikari Oe's music through my in-laws—my wife is Japanese—who are very fond of it. And I think it has a lot of depth."

And when Hikari's CDs were first released in America, several long features about the composer in major newspapers included interviews with members of the musical community. One was Seiji Ozawa, the music director of the Boston Symphony Orchestra and a family friend and Tokyo neighbor of the Oes, who told Richard Dyer of the *Boston Globe,* "I find this music of Hikari's very pure. Like Scarlatti. When a concert is finished and I come home tired, I put these recordings on; to listen to this music by Hikari Oe is good for me, a refreshment. For many years, when I was tired, I would listen to Dinu Lipatti play Myra Hess's transcription of Bach's 'Jesu, Joy of Man's Desiring,' and now I find my response to Hikari's music is similar."

In December of the following year, Mr. Ozawa was still listening to Hikari's music. "But the last time I saw Hikari himself was a few years ago, when he was younger. I had known that he was interested in music and knew that he wrote for piano, but the first time I heard his music must have been 1991 or '92. Kenzaburo Oe put a tape in my mailbox and asked my opinion. He usually delivers his new books by hand to my mailbox, especially when he's writing about his son.

"Hikari's music is very honest, not complicated. His feelings come out very straightforwardly. So the music is very straightforward, very natural, an honest expression of his feeling. He doesn't care what modern music should sound like, or whether his pieces sound like what people expect modern music to be. It's very soft and simple and naïve . . . innocent, and I enjoy it very much. Because we don't have this kind of music anymore.

"It's music you hear when you want to rest, when you are alone, you put it on your sound system, maybe have a drink before you go to bed. It calms you down, it's not exciting music. It's dangerous to talk about its simplicity or naiveness, but it's very truthful music and makes me calm. There is form, but there is not too much, and I find it refreshing that it isn't preoccupied with form. It makes me feel free; it's not composed from too much knowledge.

"And his music is as shy as he is; he's a very shy person. I haven't seen him since his CDs were so successful, but I think he must still be very shy.

"The instrumentalists on both the CDs are people I know very well. I asked how they liked it as they were learning and playing it, and they said they liked it very much. The only time I have conducted his music myself was a piece he wrote for Mstislav Rostropovich, for a concert to celebrate my sixtieth birthday. It was very well received, when I programmed that piece. We don't hear this kind of music anymore. Life is more complicated, and our music is complicated also. Rostropovich and Argerich enjoyed it, and they were smiling when playing it."

The Oes love to tell the story of that commission, which Mr. Ozawa gave Hikari when he ran into him with his mother at a neighborhood restaurant. The conductor gallantly offered to take care of the Oes' check, but they all became so absorbed in talking about the piece—and the concert—that he forgot to hand any money over to the cashier. After they left the restaurant and their paths diverged, Yukari and Hikari nearly broke into a run in their eagerness to get home and tell Kenzaburo the good news. He happened to be outside the house, and as his wife and son began jabbering simultaneously, interrupting each other in their excitement so that Kenzaburo at first wasn't sure what they were telling him, he was aware of a man who had come up behind them, appearing

THE MUSIC OF LIGHT

desperate to get a word in edgewise, muttering "Ah, excuse me—" whenever someone paused for breath, and finally, when Kenzaburo acknowledged him with a nod, presenting him, with a low bow, with the bill for three bowls of buckwheat-noodle soup. The Oes remembered the concert—which Hikari had attended with his parents—as a glorious occasion and a triumph for their old friend. They hadn't known who the pianist would be and were ecstatic when it turned out to be Martha Argerich; Hikari has felt a special affection for her ever since.

Mr. Ozawa would like to program more of Hikari's music. "Maybe with some kind of poem or narration—that can work well with piano and violin or piano and flute. Or it would be nice to schedule some narration with solo cello—maybe a reading with passages from his father's books about him. You know, I'm very happy that this young man came out in music, music that people enjoy." He was not dismayed to learn that Hikari's success was controversial. "It's O.K. to have controversy. It's lively—and brings attention to the music, which is a good thing in the end," he said.

The variety of critics' reactions to Hikari's music, which have ranged from awed praise to outright dismissal, gives a good indication of why controversy about it was inevitable. Unlike the artists who play it, whose interpretations can only be enriched by emotional involvement, critics are supposed to make their judgments in a spirit of detached objectivity. But when a composer's personal circumstances exert a strong pull on the emotions, it is scarcely possible simply to excise all knowledge of extramusical matters from the mind when evaluating his work.

In Japan, Hikari's circumstances were so well known—and his father's writings about him so widely loved—by the time his music came out that his debut could not possibly have been reviewed like any other new composer's. But reviews in America couldn't follow a conventional pattern, either. His story is simply an irresistible narrative, and critics here, though many were learning of his circumstances for the first time when they received the recordings, devoted more space to telling Hikari's tale than to describing or evaluating the music they had been assigned to review.

Feature writers could sidestep verdicts. I myself, writing at some length in the *New York Times,* praised the music but gave it only a few sentences, getting caught up in the mythic resonances of Hikari's life instead. Richard Dyer's long feature in the *Boston Globe* made no assessment, offering only Seiji Ozawa's. Teresa Watanabe, whose *Los Angeles Times* story was the most detailed article about Hikari to appear in this country, covered the question of evaluation with "Some critics call his music pure and beautiful and say that's why it sells so well. Others deem it unremarkable."

But reviewers, of course, were obliged to review the music; even so, many squeezed their assessments into a fraction of their allotted space. Their reactions ran the gamut. Anthony Liversidge, in the magazine *New Music,* gave as much space to Hikari's story as to the music itself yet plainly loved the music on its own terms:

> Oe emerges here as Mozart, Beethoven, Fauré, and Schubert reborn and rolled into one. Two remarkable sets of Hikari's small-scale compositions for piano, and later, piano and flute or violin, are jewels performed by a trio of Japanese players with directness and unassuming simplicity. If you ever wished that modern composers had the humility and courage to return to the beauty and intelligibility of classical structures, this is what you have been waiting for.

The average ratio of coverage of Hikari's story to that of his music in American reviews was about 10:1.5. And the critics who admired the music seemed to find it very difficult to do so straightforwardly.

Aaron Howard, for example, in the Houston *Herald-Voice,* wrote,

> It's clear from hearing these recordings that Oe has a great deal of musical intelligence. He's no Beethoven, but neither are 99.5 percent of professional musicians. He understands how classical music

is put together and knows how to build structures of expressiveness and intellectual satisfaction.

Some critics, like Peter M. Knapp in the *Patriot-Ledger,* seemed to want to praise the music but found themselves unable to enjoy it in musical terms. Knapp felt obliged to say that Hikari was "no Mozart or Beethoven," and "no one would argue this is great music. But it is remarkable that there is music at all from Hikari Oe, especially pieces showing such a firm grasp of fundamentals and a personal voice. These CDs represent a human triumph, and they remind us that we know very little about the workings of the mind and the act of creation."

Some, like Alan Rich in the Long Beach, California, *Press Telegram,* expressed ambivalence:

> There are two ways to approach this music. One way is to react adversely to the exploitation factor; the other is to recognize that the music is exceptionally pretty—sometimes even moving. If we can listen to Gregorian Chant out of context, there's probably nothing wrong with intruding into the private world of Hikari Oe's music, either.

And one unnamed reviewer in *Turok's Choice: The Insider's Review of New Classical Recordings* was so swayed by knowledge of Hikari's circumstances that he was unable to believe that Hikari had actually composed his work all by himself. "[The pieces] could easily pass for 'classical' pastiches, polished enough that one suspects Oe's music teacher or the (excellent) performers of helping with discreet touchup, much as Leopold Mozart did for little Wolfgang when he started composing at six."

But when they got around to judging the music, critics in this country were nearly as unanimous in discovering a few truly moving standouts among pieces that were mostly pleasant, appealing, and agreeable as they were in acknowledging that their awareness of the composer's circumstances affected their appreciation of his creations.

Four prominent American critics were invited to assess Hikari's music for this book. Only one was entirely negative: Jamie James, who currently covers classical music in New York for the London *Times* and reviews records regularly for *Stereo Review*. Considering that he is also the author of a controversial article for *Opera News* in which he claimed that popularity was a valid measure of artistic success in music, the harshness of his judgment seems surprising. But perhaps it provides additional if roundabout proof that knowledge of Hikari's circumstances affects the way his music is heard. One can only suppose he feared compromising his critical integrity by giving in to any appeal Hikari's condition might make to his kinder feelings. He said, "I hate this music," when he heard the CDs. "I find it completely suspect. It seems to me to have no emotional content at all. It's like music written by a schizophrenic trying to imitate the emotional state of a well person, music that intends to be happy rather than expressing a real emotional state. It definitely sounds like something written for beginning students—really, this sounds like a third-year flute student practicing for a recital. I heard things like this all the time when I was taking violin—they had easy sonatas beginners could learn to play. Like this, they had all the basics of classical composition but they were just exercises. Real Baroque music follows its own conventions, and it has that consistency, but it's also full of surprises. There are no surprises here. And I hate the performance, too, it's extremely metronomic, but I don't know how else you could play this, and I don't think any performance could change my mind about the music."

The other critics made thoughtful attempts to explain how and why it is difficult to simply evaluate Hikari's music *as* music. Alex Ross, the *New Yorker* music critic, offered this assessment: "A few years ago, the *New Yorker* dance critic Arlene Croce wrote a famous—to some, notorious—review of an AIDS-themed dance performance in which she declared herself incapable of reviewing the show, in fact unwilling even to attend it. Her point was that the extreme emotional content of the program—the dancers were themselves HIV-positive—made "objective" commentary impossible. Hikari Oe is a very different case, and yet I feel a sliver of the same reluctance that Croce voiced in such uncomfortably cutting terms. It's impossible to listen without thinking of Oe's mental condition: once you take that condition into account, it's impossible to assess the "objective" worth of the music. Still, I will try. I can only guess that if I had come across it at random—say, as a just-tuned-in selection on the radio—I'd have assumed it to be the childhood work of a nineteenth-century composer. It does not necessarily sound like the work of a child prodigy but, rather, the work of a very gifted youngster who found his true voice later on. So many composers' voices are "tried out" here—a bit of Bach, a bit of Mozart, a bit of Chopin or Schumann—that the original profile we customarily prize in composers seems elusive. Yet I do hear a kind of emerging personality in a minor-key piece like "Winter" or "Requiem for M" or "Siciliano"—a particular kind of static sadness that does not match the classical models. This sense of an immature, growing voice seems permanent in Oe's music. He is, perhaps, a perpetual musical adolescent.

"My assessment must look unfeeling, bloodless. Oe's achievement is, of course, staggering, once his history is taken into account. But I am unable to listen to music from that angle: I prefer to lose myself in sound, searching out aesthetic histories rather than personal ones. Much of Oe's music in an imitative Classical mode doesn't keep my ear engaged: my mind wanders to the beautifully phrased annotations by Oe's father. But certain of those moodier, more chromatic minor-key sketches have a true poetry in them, and they are haunting me as I write this in the middle of the night—haunting simply for their sound."

In 1995, when Philip Kennicott was editor of *Chamber Music* magazine, he had guessed one piece of Hikari's was by Telemann in a brief "blind" listening test. Now senior music critic of the *St. Louis Post-Dispatch,* he wrote, "Questions of quality and originality, essentially the questions of genius, stand to the side of Hikari Oe's music. Without these distractions, the listener confronts music undeveloped and raw, the elusive 1% of inspiration largely unrefined by the proverbial 99% of craft. The only judgments of quality one can make about Hikari's work is that it improves, and mere improvement is hardly a statement of worth.

"Hikari is ahistorical, and that too is discomfiting to listeners who assume reference to the past must carry ideological messages, and that innovation is meant as studied criticism of the present. His music floats through several centuries, without any apparent agenda of rehabilitation or parody. His variation style in later works reminds one of Handel's keyboard suites; his melodic ease suggests in some works Mozart, in others Schubert; his simple two-part counterpoint reminds one of Telemann.

"Yet reference is never part of a program of pastiche. Perhaps because he cannot, or perhaps because he chooses not to, what begins like Schubert often ends like Handel. His Bluebird March opens with a blustery, heavy-handed Verdi march, and then wanders off into different directions. Sometimes the movement through styles is awkward; at others it has the grace and charm of a speaker shifting languages or dialects unconsciously. Though one may hear two bars of music that seem lifted directly from a Bach two-part invention, Hikari is guilty only of the minor, unintentional stealing to which all composers are prone. A melody stored away unconsciously may come back to the composer as though fresh and self-created; the intention to steal never enters into the process of recycling.

"Our ways of speaking about music have made little space for what Hikari has produced. Approached analytically and critically, it qualifies as, at best, fluent improvisation, and improvisation is at only one remove from silence. Efforts to create for Hikari an identity which explains his music are probably wrongheaded protests against the hermetic musical world he lives in. Even Kenzaburo Oe's description of the music as "the voice of a soul wailing in darkness" tells us something about both Hikari and his composing that cannot be heard in the music. It is easy today, when confronted with a hermetic utterance—a poem, a paradox, a private monologue—to pin it down in the consciousness as the voice of a fascinating other. Kenzaburo's description draws his son's music towards the politics and literature of identity—to find a different order of value that celebrates the private, deeply personal statement simply because it speaks from outside the canon, in anger, or resistant codes.

"Yet Hikari's music doesn't belong in that category. It is not a message from outside the normative world of accepted musical standards; it is not a complaint against isolation, or a tour through the composer's distant mental universe. It is music that is spoken from silence into silence. It will entertain some, frustrate others. But perhaps it will also throw us back on that thorniest part of music we are incapable of describing, the simple monads of appealing melody, sensible harmony, and the comfortably numbing patterns of a waltz rhythm."

James R. Oestreich, classical music editor of and critic for the *New York Times,* wrote, "For what it is, Hikari Oe's music is generally well-wrought and shows a fine, understated sensibility, as in the touching little Ave Maria. What it is is rudimentary music in a Western style, which draws heavily on gestures and even specific themes of Bach, Mozart, and Beethoven.

"Mr. Oe seems to have internalized these gestures in such a way that they emerge freely and fluidly if occasionally in odd juxtapositions. He's absorbed what he's heard technically; I'm not sure he's absorbed it emotionally, but I'm not sure that matters—there isn't a lot of emotion in Boccherini's music, for example. Mr. Oe's music can at times sound like something a very young Mozart might have produced. Of course, we go to Mozart not for the ditties of his youth but for the flashes of genius, insight, and originality of his later years. Mr. Oe has not yet ventured far beyond those internalized gestures, and whether he will be able to do so seems an open question. A few transitions produce surprises, seemingly out of awkwardness rather than out of originality.

"More than anything, the music becomes wearying in quantity because of its consistently measured pace and its lack of rhythmic variety. On a deeper level, it is both unsettling and fascinating to hear a contemporary Japanese composer create afresh in a style that is so far removed from the indigenous idioms of his country and from those of his own time. Mr. Oe's work may speak to the degree to which, as has often been argued, the Western tonal system strikes a fundamental chord in the brain.

"Most of this, of course, is irrelevant to the central fact: that Mr. Oe has found a rewarding means of communication and an often charming manner of expression, which is beautifully crafted, beautifully fashioned—within the limitations of his style."

Music, like any other form of art, is meant to move, to please, to entertain. Critics are inevitably uncomfortable with the idea that part of what may move them about a work may lie outside the work itself, because they are professionally dedicated to an ideal of pure objectivity. But audiences at large do not share this ideal. And if part of what affects Hikari's audience is the knowledge that his achievements are a rare phenomenon, isn't that always part of the reason audiences enjoy the works of creative artists, or of virtuosos, for that matter? Kenzaburo once said, "Hikari composes his music in a totally detached manner, and does not create with any direct awareness of a message that he wishes to convey. However, I might point out that Hikari constantly hopes that all those around him are happy. . . . It would seem that he is striving to comfort those people in his immediate vicinity." The listeners who have been buying his discs in such extraordinary numbers all over the world surely prove that Hikari has more than succeeded in his aim.

If the musical community is not in unanimous agreement about the worth of his work, the same could be said of most contemporary composers. Nearly everyone who hears it finds at least some of his music to be both deep and beautiful, and by both commercial and critical measures, his achievements can be called brilliant. He has certainly shown flashes of real genius, and he may go on to surpass what he has created so far. But what he has already written seems likely to go on inspiring and moving listeners forever.

The Prodigious Savant

How is it possible that Hikari, so limited in some ways, unable to achieve so many of the most basic life skills of an adult, has nevertheless managed to succeed, and succeed outstandingly, in a rarefied field where critical and commercial success so seldom come together? How has he attained success of a kind that would not only be far beyond the abilities of the average person but that has

eluded so many highly gifted, highly educated, and highly motivated, disciplined, and ambitious composers?

Part of the answer to this question can be found through examining the ways the human brain processes music. When we hear
a tune, sound waves enter the ear, reaching hair-cell neurons in the
cochlea, the spiral-shaped part of the labyrinth of the inner ear.
Depending on where they are, these hair cells respond to given frequencies, high or low. They send signals up through the brainstem,
where information from both ears is processed so that we can determine where a sound is coming from. In the auditory cortex,
again, cells are specialized for high and low frequencies. This far,
the process is much the same for hearing language, music, or any
other kind of sound. But it seems to be at this point that the
process of hearing and interpreting language becomes separate
from the process of hearing and interpreting music.

It has been said that—in most people—the left hemisphere of
the brain handles language and the right hemisphere handles
music, but this is a gross oversimplification. It does seem, though,
that in general the left hemisphere specializes in the logical and
conceptual, dealing with sequential reasoning, reading and writing, mathematical computation, and comprehension of the meaning of language, and that the right hemisphere specializes in the
intuitively or directly perceived, dealing with spatial relationships,
visualization, movement, and mechanics, and with the emotional
aspects of language and their manifestations in speech.

Music has elements in common with the ways words are spoken to convey feelings: pitch, rhythm, and dynamics. Of course,
these elements are sometimes used to convey meaning, too. In
tonal languages, such as the languages spoken in China, the same
sound spoken in different pitches has entirely different meanings.
Even in English, pitch is sometimes used to convey meaning; for
example, a statement can become a question if the speaker's pitch
rises at the end.

There is a revealing passage about Hikari's speech in one of

Kenzaburo's essays: "As I listened, I was made aware of the extent to which even in everyday conversation he was careful to give a certain rhythm and overall shape to his speech. For Hikari, with his particular disability, this form and texture seem to be the fundamental principles of speech. Indeed, even when the sense of what he is saying is unclear and the syntax falls to pieces, he tends to preserve the same pattern of intonation from the beginning of his sentence to the end; in other words, for him the important thing is not so much the sense but the musicality of human speech."

Dr. Jamshed Bharucha, a cognitive psychologist at Dartmouth College, has been studying the ways the brain processes musical sound. He says that in fact both brain hemispheres contain cellular circuitry for recognizing both language and music, and that some regions of the left hemisphere specialize in music and some regions of the right specialize in language.

When I asked Dr. Bharucha how it was possible that someone with Hikari's disabilities could be so accomplished musically, he said, "This phenomenon shouldn't be surprising, because the brain is so modular and the language centers so localized. Exceptional abilities can exist in a context of compromised abilities in other areas, and Hikari Oe is apparently such a case.

"There are many more parts of the brain involved with music than with language. Music draws on several cognitive faculties. Hikari Oe's must all be intact. And this is compatible with linguistic impairment. There are areas of consonance in the brain for language and music, and most of them are not in the area of syntax but in prosody—that is, the pitch contours and rhythms of speech. So you might find that, in an individual, syntax was impaired but musical abilities were unaffected."

But combinations of abilities and disabilities comparable to Hikari's are very rare indeed. Hikari belongs to a class of people called "prodigious savants." These people are so rare, in fact, that in the past hundred years, in all the countries of the world, fewer than one hundred of them have been identified. Right now, only twenty prodigious savants are known to be alive; there are five more savants who *may* be prodigious. But no one in this tiny population of exceptional individuals has done what Hikari Oe has done. In other words, Hikari appears to be unique, the only one of his kind in the world.

People like Hikari used to be called "idiot savants," a term invented in 1887 by J. Langdon Down, for whom Down's syndrome was named. This term is now generally considered insensitive, or downright offensive, so these days such people are said to have "savant syndrome" and are known simply as "savants." The psychiatrist Darold Treffert, one of the foremost authorities on the syndrome, defines it in his book *Extraordinary People* as "an exceedingly rare condition in which persons with serious mental handicaps, either from developmental disability (mental retardation) or major mental illness (Early Infantile Autism or schizophrenia), have spectacular islands of ability or brilliance which stand in stark, markedly incongruous contrast to the handicap."

Dr. Treffert divides savants into two categories: "talented savants" and "prodigious savants." The talented savants have abilities that are remarkable in terms of their contrast to the possessor's limitations in other areas: the prodigious savants have abilities that would be remarkable even in a normal person. Hikari Oe obviously falls into this latter category.

Savant syndrome—including both the talented and the prodigious—is rare. One in every two thousand institutionalized patients with developmental disabilities has it. Some studies suggest that it is much commoner in patients with Early Infantile Autism, nearly one in ten. But such patients are very uncommon themselves; Early Infantile Autism afflicts only seven out of every hundred thousand children. (Four-fifths of children with this diagnosis are male.) The incidence of autism of all kinds is much commoner: one in every thousand births. Autism is little understood, and it is not entirely clear whether Hikari's diagnosis as autistic means that he had Early Infantile Autism (a biological condition present at birth) or simply that he had autistic symptoms, such as withdrawal and muteness (which often occur in the mentally retarded). Eighty-five percent of savants are male.

Savants usually have IQs within the range of 40–70—mildly retarded. (So "idiot savant" is something of a misnomer in any sense. At the time the term was first used, "idiot" had a precise meaning, referring to someone whose IQ was *extremely* low: below 25. Savants with IQs as low as that are almost unheard-of, even rarer than the "prodigious savants.") Normal IQ is 90–109; Hikari has an IQ of 65, falling within the "mildly retarded" classification.

Savantism takes predictable forms. The extraordinary skills of people with the syndrome tend to manifest themselves in childhood; all include phenomenal feats of memory and tend to fall within a narrow range of accomplishments: feats of memory as such (there are savants who can, for example, accurately recall a page of a city phone book thirty years after reading or hearing it read once), various forms of super-speedy mental mathematics (usually some form of calculating, especially calendar calculating—for instance, instantly and correctly naming the day of the week a given date falls on in any given year), mechanics, visual arts, and music. According to Dr. Treffert, calendar-calculating skills are the most commonly found and musical skills the next most common. All the experts on savantism agree that extraordinary musical abilities are found much more often in those whose disabilities include visual impairment (whether they are totally blind or, like Hikari, have extremely poor eyesight) than in the fully sighted. Dr. Leon Miller, an expert on specifically musical savantism, has shown that absolute pitch is more prevalent among the blind than among the sighted. It is also more common in autistic people.

As recently as 1976, a scientific study of savantism concluded that the phenomenon was an insoluble mystery, with no theory offering a satisfying explanation of how a savant's brain could work. The past two decades have seen explosive growth in our under standing of the human brain, thanks in large part to the development of sophisticated imaging techniques, and scientists now have a pretty good idea of what makes savantism possible.

While stressing that "no single theory can explain all savants," Dr. Treffert believes that cerebral lateralization—that is, the specialization of the two brain hemispheres—holds the key to the phenomenon. He introduces the relevant section of his book on savants with a description of a patient he encountered during his internship, a writer who had a malignant tumor in the right hemisphere of his brain. His one hope of survival was the removal of the entire right hemisphere—one-half of his brain. He knew that such an operation would leave him paralyzed but that his language abilities—the abilities that, as a writer, he considered essential—would not be noticeably affected. He had the hemispherectomy and was indeed paralyzed as a result, yet Dr. Treffert, who had several conversations with him afterward, could detect absolutely no change in his abilities to remember and think, and to use language.

Knowing that the specializations of the hemispheres are not absolute, Dr. Treffert conjectures that the mechanisms involved must function something like the back-up disks we make when we work on a computer. Some aspects of language processing take place in the right hemisphere, after all, yet the patient whose right hemisphere was removed appeared able to function linguistically as well as when he had it. The brain evidently *duplicates* at least some of what is needed, perhaps to increase an individual's chances of survival after head injuries.

A similar mechanism is at work in the kind of deep but narrow memory characteristic of savants. It is generally automatic, emotion-free, and based on habit and intuition rather than on rational or symbolic connections or associations; it is the kind of memory used for such poignantly pointless skills as calendar calculating. In the normal human brain, the cortico-limbic system is used for normal memory, which is cognitive and associative. But if the cortico-limbic system is damaged or defective, the cortic-striatal system, which produces the automatic memory typical of the savant, may be used instead.

Drawing on groundbreaking work on cerebral lateralization published by Norman Geschwind and Albert Galaburda in 1987, Dr. Treffert describes what he calls "the pathology of superiority." The human brain is asymmetrical, even in fetuses, with the left hemisphere usually dominant. However, while the left is usually the larger and better developed, the right dominates when humans are engaged in certain activities: most musical activities and tasks involving spatial skills. In the fetus, the right hemisphere develops before the left one does, so that there is a longer period of prenatal risk for the left. While the gonads are developing, the brains of male fetuses are flooded with testosterone (female fetuses are exposed to some testosterone, too, but most of it is converted to another hormone in the placenta). High levels of testosterone can be damaging to the brain, particularly to the left hemisphere, which is still developing at this time.

This, basically, is why certain pathologies (dyslexia, autism, delayed speech, and hyperactivity) are much more common in males than in females, and it is also why more males than females are left-handed. An excess of testosterone at this stage of fetal development can leave males more vulnerable to various physical disorders, too, especially of the immune system. If the left hemisphere is damaged, either by high testosterone levels or by actual injury to the brain, there may be a migration of neurons to the right hemisphere, which then grows larger and becomes the dominant hemisphere in the affected individual. This is the result of "compensatory growth leading to superior development of some portions of the brain as a result of poorer development in other portions," as Dr. Treffert puts it.

Geschwind and Galaburda also pointed out that the brain of a normal fetus (in various other species in addition to our own) has many surplus neurons that die immediately before the fetus is born. If the left hemisphere is damaged or injured, the right hemisphere can draw, as it were, on its extra neurons, which then do not die off as they would in normal development. Interestingly, a disproportionate number of savants were born prematurely—not Hikari though. But Hikari's left hemisphere was certainly damaged—dramatically so.

And Hikari, in addition to the normal complement, had a special surplus of brain cells. He was actually born with two separate brains, a fact that his family apparently did not discover until he was in his late teens. After his violent episodes, they took him for hospital examinations so that doctors could try to determine whether the physical causes of his seizures might also be responsible for the changes in his behavior. In the course of these consultations, one of the doctors conducting the tests mentioned that the lump protruding from Hikari's skull when he was born had actually contained a separate, nonfunctioning brain. So Hikari was at one stage of his development endowed with far more brain cells—twice as many, possibly—than a normal baby, though the relevance of this phenomenon to Hikari's present condition is unclear.

In an entirely factual episode in his partly fictionalized memoir of Hikari, Kenzaburo recalled being amazed at learning of this for the first time so late in Hikari's life. He certainly did not remember its being mentioned when Hikari was born, nor did Yukari. In a taxi on the way home from the hospital, he asked her whether the doctor had told Hikari that he had an extra brain. Hearing the question, Hikari made a characteristic joke. At that time, a Japanese bookstore had an attention-getting television commercial in which a child, wearing a straw hat, was shown with his beautiful young mother; then the child was shown as a grownup young man, looking up at the sky and asking whatever had happened to that straw hat of his childhood—"Where is the hat I had in those days?" Mimicking the words of the commercial, Hikari asked whatever could have happened to the brain he had in those days. (Kenzaburo explained that Hikari knew very well that it is grotesque to compare a brain to a hat, and that he was using that knowledge deliberately in making the joke.) Kenzaburo told him that it was dead but, wanting to put a positive spin on it, pointed out that it was surely a good thing to have had two brains, and Hikari cheerfully agreed.

"And now you must take good care of the brain you have left, and live to a ripe old age," Kenzaburo told him.

"Sibelius lived to be ninety-two, Scarlatti ninety-nine, and Eduardo di Capua a hundred and two!" Hikari happily recited. The cab driver asked about the last of these names, and Hikari explained that he was the composer of "O Sole Mio."

In his discussion of the extra neuronal cells that die before a baby is born, Dr. Treffert describes the work of Dr. Brent Logan, who directs the Prenatal and Infant Education Institute in Snohomish, Washington. Dr. Logan has investigated the effects of prenatal exposure to certain stimuli, one of which is classical music, in the belief that using some of the doomed extra cells will cause them not to die off but to be retained, resulting in increased intelligence in the baby after it is born. This is because when these cells receive stimulation, they begin to develop the synapses that connect them to one another, and it is only the neuronal cells that have not developed such connections that nature has programmed to die.

In a telephone interview in the spring of 1997, Dr. Treffert said that when he first described this work, he was skeptical, feeling that as of the time Dr. Logan presented his findings, in 1986, they had not been tested in any conclusive way. Yet since then, Dr. Treffert said, studies investigating these theories of prenatal development have produced more convincing results, leading him to wonder whether Yukari Oe's steady diet of Western classical music while pregnant with Hikari may have contributed to her son's exceptional musical skills.

Other factors also play a part in the development of savant skills. One is sensory deprivation. This is particularly true for musical savants, who tend disproportionately to be both autistic and visually impaired—many are totally blind. Very often, they have other physical handicaps, too. The role of visual impairment is obvious: much greater concentration on aural stimuli is possible where there are no visual stimuli to compete with them for someone's attention. It is also, of course, advantageous, for someone who cannot see can use the sense of hearing as a substitute for sight in many ways. (As a small child, before getting eyeglasses, Hikari was nearly blind.)

In one of the essays in *A Healing Family,* Kenzaburo speculates that Hikari's poor vision led him to develop the habit of using auditory cues to recognize people instead of visual ones. He recounts something Hikari said while the family was listening to many violin recordings, trying to choose a violinist to record the music on Hikari's second CD. Yukari and Mr. Okano asked Hikari for his impressions of Tomoko Kato's playing. "Very beautiful," he said, "but I don't know what her voice looks like." At first they thought he must be speaking of some quality of her violin playing, but it later became clear that he meant he had never heard her speaking voice, and that he thinks of human voices as having distinctive "looks." In the same essay, Kenzaburo tells of an occasion when the novelist Shohei Ooka, an older writer whom he now says he "respected as more than a friend," once called the house and Hikari answered the phone. He told his parents, "Mr. Ooka is a note low today." And in fact, Ooka was very ill: he had been calling Kenzaburo to tell him he was going into a hospital for tests, and that afternoon, at the hospital, he died.

The neurologist L. S. Vygotsky wrote, speaking of his work with deaf and blind children, "A handicapped child represents a qualitatively different, unique type of development. If a blind or deaf child achieves the same level of development as a normal child, then the child with a defect achieves this in another way, by another course, by other means. . . . This uniqueness transforms the minus of the handicap into the plus of compensation."

The role of autism in making savant skills possible is similar.

An autistic person's experiences are highly restricted. Dr. Bernard Rimland, who has studied such skills in the autistic, stresses the importance of their inability to choose or discriminate among their reactions to stimuli.

Normal children who like music, for example, may choose when they hear something pleasing or interesting on the radio to ignore everything else around them and concentrate on listening to it, and such concentration will be a deliberately cultivated skill that improves each time they practice it. Or they may choose to give some of their attention to it intermittently, since there are many other things that interest them in their environment. An autistic child, if music is one of the things that fall within the narrow range of what he responds to, will concentrate helplessly on it. He won't have to decide not to pay attention to the potential distractions around him: his mother's voice, the food on a nearby table, the antics of the family dog, or even to a wide range of thought, memories, and images that the music itself might suggest to someone who was open to them. Such things are in a very real sense simply not there for him. Dr. Rimland compares this to operating with a dial stuck in one position: an autistic person may be able to take in only one kind of stimulus (or one of a very small number), and he can take it in only with total intensity, like a radio receiver locked to get only one station, always at top volume.

The restrictedness and intensity of interests that characterize the autistic can certainly facilitate the mastery of information within a limited field. In another entirely factual passage in the same memoir, Kenzaburo described Hikari's newspaper-reading habits. He said Hikari would open the paper every morning and turn straight to the obituaries. Originally, he was interested in finding out whether anyone in the musical world had died, but as he got into the habit of scanning these columns, he took to reading death notices about people in any field, and he became fascinated with the statistics more or less for their own sake: the causes of the deaths reported and the ages at which people died. "When-

ever he comes across a new disease," his father wrote, "he memo-
rizes the characters. He asks me or my wife how they are pronounced, then takes a breath, and *pronounces* them with emotion:
'Aah! This many people died today, too! Acute pneumonia, 89
years old; heart attack, 69; bronchial pneumonia, 83. . . . Aha!
This person was a pioneering researcher in blowfish poisoning!
Arterial thrombosis, 74; lung cancer, 86, . . . ah! This many people died again!'"

Many musical savants have physical handicaps, but it is not
clear what these disabilities have to do with their skills. The handicaps may be simply a contributing factor in reinforcing the nar-
rowness of their interests: people for whom movement is difficult
or awkward may not care to venture far beyond the piano or the
stereo, for example. They know they can enjoy themselves there,
after all, and the outside world is full of pitfalls. In Hikari's case, a
combination of poor coordination and extremely bad eyesight
have obviously always made sedentary pursuits more inviting
than active ones. His mother has said that when he is walking in
the street, a shadow cast by a telephone pole will look like rising
stairs to him because of his lack of depth vision, and he can be sure
he is walking on level ground only by feeling it underfoot. And
since his teens, the ever-present danger of a seizure has given him
another reason to limit his activities.

Another factor involved in the formation of savant skills is
the enormous amount of admiring attention they receive. If the
drive to earn the approval of others can motivate even highly intelligent people to surpass themselves and master very difficult
skills, imagine what a strong motivating factor it would be in the
case of someone who is in general regarded as a liability, a dependent nuisance requiring endless care and attention he can neither
earn nor reciprocate. If such a person has just one means of es-
caping that category, one can understand very well why he would
cultivate it tirelessly. And there are numerous cases where savant
skills have emerged as their possessors were increasingly re-

warded for having them, and some cases where savant skills have disappeared when their possessors found other means of winning approval. Yet the role of positive reinforcement is in a sense relatively minor, because no amount of it can produce such skills if the brain is not somehow physically equipped to handle the tasks involved.

Musical Savants

Before Hikari, it was thought that musical savants did not have the capacity to create. The earliest well-documented case of musical savantism was an American slave, Thomas Greene Bethune, born in 1849. When his "master," Colonel Bethune, bought his mother at an auction in 1850, her baby son (the youngest of her fourteen children) was included in the sale for free, since he was blind, and a blind slave was automatically deemed useless. As a toddler, he startled people around him by his accurate mimicking of bird calls. More remarkable skills were evident before he was four years old. One night Colonel Bethune, walking by the room where his piano was kept, heard little Tom accurately playing a Mozart sonata that his own daughter had been practicing. The boy played other pieces by ear on his owner's piano. By the time he was six years old, he could play anything he had heard once, unhesitatingly and without mistakes, although he seemed unable to learn anything non-musical. Like Hikari's, his early speech consisted of repeating what he heard. Later, one of the skills he exhibited on stage was repeating long texts after hearing them only once. They might be in abstruse English or in foreign languages he did not know; he plainly did not understand what they meant but mimicked the sounds exactly. He could also sing any song in any language after a single hearing.

Colonel Bethune hired musicians to play pieces so Tom could learn them and add them to his repertoire. At seven, he knew three thousand of them and began concertizing; his highly successful performing career, touring all over America and Europe, continued throughout his life, although he was judged mentally incompetent by American courts in 1879 and 1886. Of course, his guardians stood to gain by such judgments, since they would then be able to take complete charge of his not inconsiderable income. (His performances at age seven alone netted $100,000.) Even when that is taken into account, it is clear that Blind Tom, as he was known, was mentally retarded, though contemporary accounts of him vary to an extent that makes it impossible to form a precise notion of his limitations. He appears never to have mastered ordinary social interactions, and there are many accounts of his odd mannerisms, such as twirling about on one foot while listening to music, grimacing, and bursting out laughing at inappropriate times. (He also had the endearing habit of heartily applauding his own performances.) His language skills were decidedly limited. He was said to know fewer than 100 words but more than five thousand piano pieces. Besides playing Bach, Beethoven, Chopin, Mendelssohn, and many other composers, he could improvise in a wide range of styles.

When he was eleven, he was invited to perform at the White House for President James Buchanan. Some musicians who had caught his act suspected that some trickery might be involved, so they came to his hotel room with a test they had devised. One played an original composition, thirteen pages long, that Tom could have had no chance of hearing previously. He reproduced it, accurately and effortlessly, after hearing it once. Another musician went on to play a twenty-page original composition, and Tom had no trouble playing that, too. On later tours, in Europe, he was subjected to further tests, and experts there ascertained that he had perfect pitch.

While he could improvise in any style he was familiar with (and he needed only a single hearing for familiarization) and was a spectacularly successful performer, he did not compose pieces in the same sense that Hikari Oe does. Blind Tom's improvisations obviously entertained audiences as demonstrations of skill in a performing situation. Hyperbolically enthusiastic contemporary accounts of him make it plain that audiences were very much impressed, but there is nothing to suggest that his improvisations were moving—or valued—as works of art. At any rate, they had no life apart from Blind Tom's performing career. Most musical savants cannot improvise at all, though, and in fact most savants show no creativity whatsoever in any field.

Blind Tom's career came to a pathetically abrupt end in 1902, when he was fifty-three. Colonel Bethune died, and Tom simply could not learn to function without him. He died six years later, poor, forgotten, and alone.

Another American musical savant is known in the literature as Harriet G. Hers was one of the first documented cases of musical savantism in a female; female musical savants are even more unusual than female savants in general. Born in Boston in 1916, Harriet was the sixth in a family of seven children. Her mother was a voice coach. Shortly before Harriet was born, her eldest sister had been injured in an accident. In consequence, her mother became almost frantically anxious to protect the new baby, so she kept Harriet's crib near her in the studio where she gave lessons. Being busy with her students, she gave the baby very little attention; the early stimuli in the infant's life consisted almost entirely of the sounds of the piano and of human voices singing. Harriet never smiled and almost never cried—and when she did cry, her mother could always silence her instantly by playing the piano, as Hikari at the same age could be quieted with classical records.

One night Harriet's father walked by the studio and heard someone singing "Caro Nome," a difficult, showy soprano aria from *Rigoletto*. It sounded like one of his wife's students, a professional singer who was learning the piece at the time. Surprised that she should be practicing so late, he looked in to find that the singer was his tiny daughter, warbling away in her crib. The account is reminiscent of Colonel Bethune's nocturnal wanderings bringing Blind Tom's talents to light, but Harriet's feat was even more astonishing than Tom's: she was seven months old at the time.

When Harriet was two, her mother gave birth to another daughter, this one with a club foot, and the new baby usurped Harriet's specially protected status. Harriet no longer lived isolated in the studio, and she was ill-prepared for being thrown all of a sudden into the rough-and-tumble melee of family life with her five older siblings. They picked on her, and she did her best to torment them in return, breaking their toys, attacking their pets, and constantly thumping out rhythms with a stick. She could not speak but effortlessly learned to play the various musical instruments she found around the house: by the time she was four, she had mastered the violin, trumpet, clarinet, and French horn.

At the same age, she was apparently tortured beyond endurance by hearing the mistakes a student of her mother's was making in her attempts to learn the "Bell Song" from *Lakmé*. When the student sang the same note flat for a third time, little Harriet barreled into the studio, head down, and butted the student in the stomach, forcing her out the door! Not long after that, her brothers and sisters discovered that they could torment her by hitting a stubbornly out-of-tune note on the piano they used for practice. Harriet would try to butt them off the piano bench, but one would continue sounding the note while the others held Harriet back. One day when they had gone away and left the keyboard unlocked, Harriet ripped out the key—and its hammer.

By the time she was seven, she could accompany her mother's students with the skill of a professional and could outperform even her most talented older siblings on both piano and violin. She still could not speak and had resisted all attempts to toilet-train her. But little by little she began reproducing the sounds of words as if they were music, and she gradually learned to speak in this way by the time she was nine. Her father, a mechanic, sometimes took her to the garage where he worked; soon she learned the names for all the makes and models of cars she saw there, as well as the names of their parts. She had perfect pitch, and her memory for anything she had ever heard appeared to be flawless. Her father once read her the first three pages of the Boston telephone book, and for several years afterward she was able to supply the correct number for any of the names on those pages. She could also do calendar calculating, but only within a fifty-five-year period. (When she was asked how many weeks there were in a year, though, she answered, "Forty-eight.") All her life, she could correctly recite the weather report of any day she'd lived through, however many years ago it was, and in fact she seemed to remember everything she had ever experienced, though she never showed emotion in her account of a day's events, even if they had been traumatic, unless they involved music.

When she was nine, having finally been toilet-trained and learned to speak, she was sent to school and placed in a special-education class, but she was so unteachable and uncontrollable that she stopped going after two months. Two years later, she tried again and stayed until she was sixteen. Her IQ was 73. She could read music, although she had never been taught to, but she could not define words or do arithmetic, and she was completely incapable of abstract reasoning. She never knew who was president or how many inches there were in a yard, yet her knowledge of music was encyclopedic, not only of its academic or performing aspects but also of gossip about classical-music personalities. She displayed emotion only when talking about music. She would recount an opera plot, for example, and display tenderness, delight, or terror as appropriate. Yet one Christmas day, showing no emotion at all, she told her family that she had dreamed her father died; it was the first time she ever described having a dream. Hours later, he did die, and Harriet calmly sat down to eat while the body was being carried out of the grief-stricken house.

Her musical talents were breathtaking. She could not only improvise in the style of any composer she'd ever heard but could even improvise with the right hand playing in the style of one composer and the left hand, simultaneously, in the style of another. Yet despite her improvisational skills, she never seemed to feel the urge to create new music for its own sake, although she embellished and varied pieces she knew. She could also identify virtually any piece in the standard classical repertory after hearing a few measures of it, and could usually supply the opus number and the year it was composed, just as Hikari can produce the Köchel number after hearing a bar or two of anything by Mozart. When Harriet was eighteen, her younger sister, Mary, got her a job making salads in the kitchen of a hospital. Harriet's life skills were so inadequate that Mary had to accompany her for the first six months before Harriet could manage to get to work, do her job, and go home again on her own. Once established in her routine, Harriet coped by following it inflexibly.

She held this job until she was forty and was considered completely reliable. She always saved half of her disposable income and spent the other half on classical music, records, and concert tickets. For twenty years, she attended every Saturday evening concert of the Boston Symphony Orchestra. She also accompanied her mother's students, and, like Hikari, spent all her leisure time listening to music.

When Harriet was forty, she injured her foot and was unable to go to work for a while. Her psyche never recovered from this disruption of her routine, and she was admitted to the same hospital where she had worked, this time as a patient. Disoriented, delusional, and depressed, she was diagnosed as psychotic. She never recovered.

Another American musical savant, Leslie Lemke, is among the most famous savants alive. His performances have given him wide international exposure; he is the subject of both a television drama and a documentary film. Born in Wisconsin, in 1952, he was a premature baby, given up for adoption at birth. His eyes were removed surgically because he had a condition called retrolental fibroplasia, in which the eye may actually burst in the socket. After spending the first half-year of his life in an institution, the Milwaukee Children's Home, he was adopted by May and Joe Lemke. His adoptive mother was fifty-two, but she cared for him with energetic devotion. He needed it. Besides being blind, the boy proved to be both spastic—he had cerebral palsy—and, like most musical savants, mildly retarded. (His IQ is 58.) Rather than speaking, he repeated what he heard—sometimes a whole day's worth of overheard conversation—verbatim.

Because he seemed interested in sound and rhythm, his mother, like Hikari's, thought that teaching him to play the piano might provide a kind of therapy for him, and bought one when he was seven. He learned it quickly, and by the time he was ten he could also play the ukelele, the concertina, the xylophone, and bongo drums, although he had not learned to dress or to feed himself.

But the scope of his talents was not apparent until his early teens, when one night after his family had been watching a movie on television that featured Tchaikovsky's Piano Concerto no. 1 as its theme, his mother heard that music playing and thought she had forgotten to turn off the television. But it was Leslie. He had never heard it before, but he was playing the piano part—perfectly. (One cannot help noticing that his special skill was discovered exactly as Blind Tom's and Harriet's had been. The revelation of Hikari Oe's musical talent does not follow the same dramatic pattern, but his father's mistaking his identification of the bird call for his own memory of the announcer's voice on the record is similar.)

Leslie Lemke began performing in public in 1974, when he was twenty-two, and has been doing it ever since, amazing audiences with skills that seem very similar to those of Blind Tom. He has performed live all over America and on many nationally broadcast television shows. He has also given concerts in many countries in Europe and Asia.

He plays the pieces in his repertory generally using only nine fingers, because he can barely use the little finger on his left hand. He sings, too, not only in English but also in languages he does not know. His act concludes with a session in which the audience is invited to play or sing anything at all for him to reproduce at once—which he always does, faithfully, including any mistakes the audience member may have made. After doing so, he proceeds to play or sing variations on the piece until someone intervenes to stop him. He has reproduced taped operas nearly an hour in length, playing the piano and singing in foreign languages.

At first, people would call out requests to him, but it soon became clear that Leslie was absolutely compelled to play a song all the way through once he had heard its name: concerts were sometimes prolonged until two or three in the morning as he worked his way, in order, through all the titles he had heard. Now, requests are submitted in writing, and someone reads Leslie a manageable number of them. Tchaikovsky's Piano Concerto no. 1 is still in his repertory, and whenever he plays it (unless someone stops him), he begins by mimicking the television announcer's voice from the evening of the first time he heard it, telling the audience that tonight's movie is "Sincerely Yours," starring Dorothy Malone and Basil Rathbone. And his speech still consists largely of repeating what he has heard.

When Leslie was thirty-three, his mother developed Alzheimer's disease and went to live with her older daughter, while Leslie moved in with her younger one, Mary. No one was confident that Leslie would be able to cope with this transition, since he had been so completely and exclusively dependent on May, but he adjusted very well. His sister took her mother's place with Leslie, giving him loving care and encouragement both at home and on his concert tours, and she established an organization called Miracle of Love Ministries, which presents Leslie's concerts—usually free—at churches, schools, prisons, and nursing homes as well as at conventional venues.

Leslie has made up at least one song, "Down on the Farm in Arpin" (Arpin is the town where he lived with his parents). Dr. Treffert has heard this song and has also listened, often, to a tape of Hikari Oe's music that some friends brought him after a visit to Japan. "Leslie's song is just a little ditty," he said. "I don't want to put it down, but it sounds like pieces of other things I've heard. Hikari Oe's music is something else. I listen to that tape over and over. It's become my favorite music—one of my favorite things to listen to, anyway. Leslie Lemke is not a composer in anything like the sense Hikari is. Leslie's song is really just variations on a theme." Improvisation is one of Lemke's performing skills, and he remembers his improvisations as he remembers all the music he has ever heard.

The three lives just described demonstrate that musical savantism tends to follow a pattern. Interest in music manifests itself at an early age, with skills often springing out full-blown. Oliver Sacks has written that "savant gifts . . . do not seem to develop as normal talents do. They are fully fledged from the start." Hikari's case is exceptional in this as in several other respects: the most striking difference between his first and his second CD is the greater depth and complexity of some of the pieces.

Sometimes the interest in music seems to exist in a vacuum, with the child taking no interest in anything else. A female American musical savant with an IQ so low that it was difficult to test had such a limited attention span that she could never watch an entire episode of *Sesame Street,* yet she sat rapt through a television broadcast of *Peter Grimes,* a piece that even many opera-loving adults do not consider notably accessible. In Hikari's case, he would listen attentively to classical music for hours at a time when he was still a toddler, when nothing else, with the exception of birdsong, could engage his attention at all. "We did not think he would ever be capable of human communication," his father said. Oliver Sacks has written that "savant talents do not seem to connect, as normal talents do, to the rest of the person. . . . this is strongly suggestive of a neural mechanism different from that which underlies normal talents."

Most musical savants are very slow in learning to speak, and their early attempts at speech tend to be "echolalic"—that is, they repeat what they have just heard, with little or no evidence of understanding. In some cases, they never really learn to speak at all, and in nearly all cases, their language skills are far below average. They very frequently show autistic symptoms at an early age. And in most cases (as with the majority of savants in all categories), their IQ scores fall within the "mildly retarded" range. Hikari Oe follows this classic pattern.

Virtually all musical savants have absolute pitch, as Hikari does. And while they may learn other instruments, sometimes mastering a number of them almost effortlessly, their primary instrument is almost always the piano. The piano is not the only instrument Hikari can play, but the accordion is also a keyboard instrument, and while he has played bongos, he doesn't seem

much interested in them, and has never written for percussion instruments. Although most of the music he has written is for the
piano, he has also written for the flute (his recorded music is for a
Western flute, but he has written for the shakuhachi, a Japanese
flute, too), violin, viola, and cello.

According to some studies, a large proportion of musical savants have musically talented relatives (as Hikari has), so that some
psychologists feel there is the possibility of a genetic component in
their abilities. That theory is controversial, though, and some recent studies have suggested that this is not the case.

Of all the cases discovered through searching the literature on
savants and interviewing experts in the field, the three musical savants described above were the ones who resembled Hikari most
closely. Yet, although all of them could and did improvise, Hikari
is the only savant whose skill is composing. He is also the only savant whose musical creativity is independent of performing skills.
(There are other musical savants without performing skills, but
their musical interests are passive; they neither sing nor play instruments, but listening to music is the only thing that interests
them, and the skills that qualify them for savant status involve
their phenomenal abilities in remembering the music they have
heard.) Oliver Sacks has characterized savant talents, contrasting
them with normal talents, as having a "peculiar isolation, uninflu-
enceability, and automaticity." By such a definition, Hikari seems
to be the only savant whose savant talent has manifested itself in
an unsavantlike way.

Dr. Treffert is considered the preeminent expert on savantism
in this country. He has written a definitive book on savants and is
currently working on another, which will include material on
Hikari. "There are other savants who may do some composing, but
it's pretty primitive," he says. "Their compositions are variations
on some theme they've heard. They are definitely not creating in
the sense that he is. I think I know about all the savants by now,
and I'd say Hikari is absolutely unique."

Sources of Creativity

Why has Hikari been able to transcend the usual savant limitations? Dr. Oliver Sacks has written movingly of the creativity involved in the brain adaptations that make such phenomena as savant skills possible: "Defects, disorders, diseases . . . can play a paradoxical role, by bringing out latent powers, developments, evolutions, forms of life, that might never be seen, or even be imaginable, in their absence. It is the paradox of disease, in this sense, its 'creative potential.'" And he appears to share the views of Hans Asperger, one of the first to identify autism, about the existence of a specifically autistic kind of intelligence: "a sort of intelligence scarcely touched by tradition and culture—unconventional, unorthodox, strangely 'pure' and original, akin to the intelligence of true creativity."

But it is the disease itself that is creative, not the diseased. Dr. Sacks agrees with others who have studied savant phenomena that, generally speaking, savants have little creativity in the sense in which the term is usually understood. In fact, "absence of creativity" is part of the definition of savant skills. In *Extraordinary People,* Dr. Treffert poses the question, "Is the savant creative?" and answers, "Not very. . . . In general, savants echo rather than create, and mimic rather than invent." Today, he says, "Someone like Hikari Oe challenges all the assumptions about savants not having creativity. The reason that savants are not very creative is that they must use more primitive circuitry in terms of the parts of the cortex that are involved. That's what accounts for the kinds of memories they have—their deep but not wide recall. Hikari Oe demonstrates a crossover from the basic to the more advanced circuitry—that is, the higher cortical circuitry. His case proves that there can be a crossover, that there's not necessarily a strict dichotomy between basic preserved circuitry and the kind of higher advanced circuitry that is absent in many savants. In order to be creative, an individual has to be able to tap this higher circuitry and memory, and in Hikari's case, apparently, complex emotions as well. My idea of savants having two dichotomous circuits, and being reliant on more primitive circuits because the higher ones are damaged, is something Hikari challenges. He proves that the dichotomy is not as absolute as I might have thought, but, rather, a relative thing."

Dr. Leon Miller, the preeminent American expert on specifically musical savants, said, "Hikari Oe is unique in several respects.

There are a few other musical savants with compositional predilec-tions—they are few and far between—but Hikari Oe is remark-able in terms of his compositional style, in a practical sense. The others make music sitting down at a keyboard; Hikari thinks it up and writes it down."

He compared Hikari to a savant called Eddie (whose training Dr. Miller discussed extensively in his book, *Musical Savants*): "I tried Eddie on musical notation for some time, but he was so in-terested in the productive aspect of music that he found it excru-ciatingly slow. And other nondisabled musicians with absolute pitch could be whizzes at dictation, but their oral skills always slowed down their progress in reading. They were impatient, they found it too laborious. It sounds like the absolute opposite with Hikari—more comprehensive knowledge, less productive knowledge. His history makes a good argument for the impor-tance of early learning by looking and listening. There's a popu-lar notion that learning is intention-centered and needs a lot of deliberate rehearsals, many instances of producing an overt re-sponse that the environment can correct—those arguments usu-ally come from cognitive psychologists who work with computer programs." But understanding music is one thing, and creating it is another.

Pressed about creativity in musical savants, Dr. Miller said, "I have difficulty responding to questions about creativity, about how unusual it is for savants to be creative. 'Creativity' is a slippery, nasty term. What is it? You and I are being creative as we talk to each other now; this is what a colleague of mine here calls 'mun-dane creativity.' That's a kind of creativity we don't pay attention to, because it comes so naturally to us.

"And in addition to the problem of defining 'creativity,' there is another problem, which has to do with trying to distinguish competence from opportunity: whether or not the compositional talent has been fostered in the savant musician. Typically, it has not been fostered or it may never have emerged because the savant's needs are so particular, and the particular kind of pedagogical environment that would be required to develop such abilities has never been supplied." Dr. Miller has attended symposiums on savant musicianship where it was agreed that savants require a rethinking of pedagogical style.

Savants tend to be rigid and inflexible. Think of Harriet G., able to live the semblance of a normal life only by rote mastery of a routine. She was utterly—and permanently—unhinged when her routine was disrupted. Think, too, of Leslie Lemke, whose life is playing the piano, yet who never just sits down and plays; he needs to be prompted somehow before he will set his fingers on the keys. And once he hears a prompt, he appears to be incapable of varying his reaction to it. Think of his inability to disregard a request, continuing to play for ten or twelve hours or more, working his way through the list he has helplessly memorized.

There is, in fact, one theory that the remarkable memory skills savants display should not be seen as an ability to remember an extraordinary quantity of information but as an inability to forget it. Dr. Sacks described a musical savant called Martin A. as a "Walking Grove"—after hearing his father read all nine volumes of the 1954 *Grove Dictionary of Music and Musicians,* he was able to recite the whole thing, and always did so in an imitation of his father's voice.

Cases such as his appear to support a theory advanced by the Nobel laureate Francis Crick with Graeme Mitchison: dreaming enables the brain to forget—or, more explicitly, to sort information in terms of whether or not it should be retained, rather like clearing unneeded files from a computer's hard disk. According to this theory, we need to sort because our cortexes are too small to retain all the information we take in. Nearly all mammals have rapid eye movement (REM) sleep, the kind of sleep in which dreaming takes place. The spiny anteater of Australia is an exception; its cortex is disproportionately large in relation to the animal's overall size.

Savants probably dream, but they certainly do not recall or report dreams as normal people do. Harriet G., for example, spoke of having a dream only once in her life. The nature of savant dreaming has not received much scientific study: a pair of calendar-calculating twin savants were observed to have more or less normal REM sleep. But if dreaming really is part of a forgetting process that involves prioritizing, the savant's apparent lack of access to whatever dreams he may have is obviously relevant to the savant's typical lack of creativity, which, in turn, is an aspect of the savant's typical inability to prioritize, or use judgment about the relative importance of various elements.

Does Hikari dream? The question has become part of a standard talk Kenzaburo gives when introducing concerts of Hikari's music. Since he was a child, the Oes have patiently tried to find out, explaining to Hikari what a dream is and asking if he has ever had one. But he has never given them a satisfying answer.

It is clear that Hikari, like most musical savants, remembers any music that interests him. Extramusical memories are another matter. His ability to retain most nonmusical information is limited. A striking anecdote in Kenzaburo's memoir of Hikari suggests that—unlike, say, Harriet G.—he remembers nonmusical images that aroused strong emotions. An American graduate student was visiting the family in 1990 in the course of completing a thesis on Oe and Mishima. With her, Kenzaburo discovered, to his distress, that Hikari could remember seeing a photograph of Mishima's severed head just after that author's spectacular suicide. He was only seven at the time, just beginning to speak and as yet barely able to communicate at all, but he had retained that horrifying image for twenty years. Kenzaburo worried about its being material for nightmares but acknowledged that he has no way of knowing whether Hikari has nightmares, or, indeed, any dreams at all.

Another anecdote in Kenzaburo's memoir suggests that, whether or not he has experienced them, Hikari has come to understand what dreams are. One fall, the family had planned to go to a cottage in Izu, a popular resort south of Mt. Fuji, for a vacation, but a typhoon struck, and they canceled the plan. But Hikari was so determined to go anyway that Kenzaburo could not bear to disappoint him, and the two of them set off together on the train despite the weather. When they reached the cottage, they lit a fire and stretched out on futons near the fireplace. Kenzaburo thought Hikari had fallen asleep, while he himself, half drunk and half asleep, brooded on gloomy thoughts inspired by a book he had been reading about William Blake. As he lay there, muttering unhappily, he was startled to feel Hikari's hand touching him tenderly. "It's all right, it's all right," Hikari said. "It's only a dream, there's nothing to worry about because it's only a dream."† And Hikari has called one of his pieces "Dream"—his first composition for violin, written in 1993 (though he invented its opening while still in his teens).

There are many theories about the purposes of dreams, and none has been accepted as conclusive. But most psychologists agree that dreams are probably somehow useful in sorting things out unconsciously. And one of the most striking peculiarities of the savant mind is its ability to sort information unconsciously, its intuitive grasp of rules that the normal mind would not be able to implement without conscious understanding. Dr. Treffert discusses at some length a matter that has intrigued all the experts on savantism: the musical savant's apparent access to the underlying rules of music, an access that seems almost magical given the savant's inability to conceptualize these rules.

One theory that might account for savant musical abilities was expounded by Howard Gardner in a book called *Frames of Mind,* published in 1983. He argued that our abilities might be less interdependent than has usually been supposed, so that rather than conceiving of individuals as having more or less of some quality called "intelligence," we should think in terms of six separate intelligences: linguistic, musical, logico-mathematical, spatial,

†Translation by Yoshiko Kuwahara.

bodily-kinesthetic, and personal. In any given individual, some of these might be very highly developed, some much less so.

Nonsavant musicians certainly vary widely in the ways they consciously grasp what they are doing and in their abilities to verbalize what they do. Dr. Miller says, "One of the problems that the musical savant has is describing what he's about. The difficulty arises because he has to describe it using a nonmusical language. But it isn't clear whether this difficulty reflects a specific language deficit or a more general conceptual problem, or whether it's something about music itself—music is kind of ineffable, it's hard to talk about, you just do it. One of the things I have found about the folks I have interviewed is that their talking about what they do in music is not very informative. And if you take a look at the literature on composition, often composers who don't have disabilities aren't clear on what they do anyway. So you have to separate the problems of the genre from problems of communication. Composing is a kind of litmus test for getting savant behavior the attention it deserves, rescuing it from the backwater of intelligent activities. The fact is, if any of these guys can do these things as well—within certain constraints—as people with normal I.Q.s, we have to rethink our models of intelligent human behavior, because the models we have now do not accommodate a phenomenon like Hikari Oe."

Hikari is strikingly different from other musical savants. Most are notably deficient in the ability to conceptualize *anything*. Even when their verbal scores in intelligence testing are on the high end of the "mildly retarded" range, they may actually score a zero in the portions of the test devoted to abstract reasoning. When Leslie Lemke was given a test involving fitting blocks of given shapes into the appropriate holes on a board (a kind of test where his blindness would be no disadvantage), he was unable to do it: the testers' conclusion was that "abstract ability is essentially absent." Harriet G.'s psychiatrist, Dr. D. S. Viscott, reported that she was unable to answer any questions about how things are alike or dissimilar. "No amount of pressure would make her say anything ex-

cept "a nickel is a nickel and a dime is a dime. They are not alike at
all." She could, however, make sophisticated analytical comparisons of music.

Hikari does have the ability to conceptualize, but his difficulties in communicating indicate that this ability is limited. Naturally, he is able to communicate well about music, especially with
fellow musicians, since the givens of their conversations are mutually understood. The shortcomings in his manner of communicating about nonmusical matters seem to involve a lack of
understanding of others' needs. Autistic people often fail to explain
things sufficiently, as though assuming that anything they know
must be known to everyone else, too, one of the peculiar features of
autism being a lack of the usual sense of "self" and "others."

In an essay, Kenzaburo has described Hikari's tendency to
leave out, in speech, the thing he is talking about, illustrating this
with an example: Hikari once asked, at a medical examination,
"Next month, which is April, will be so kind as to continue?" But
continue *what?* He didn't say. His parents were able to figure out
what he meant, because they knew something the examining doctor didn't: some of Hikari's teachers at Karasuyama were leaving
that March—not continuing to work with him—so Hikari wondered whether the doctor would stop working with him then, too.
His father notes that this sort of communication, with the premise
left out, is possible in a family, where the members recognize one
another's references and do not need to have them spelled out, but
it is impossible when talking to outsiders. He goes on to wonder
whether, in accompanying Hikari and interpreting for him to facilitate his dealings with the outside world, his family has prevented him from improving his communication skills "by
depriving him of the need to make a linguistic effort."

As Dr. Sacks has described them, the autistic artist Stephen
Wiltshire's shortcomings in verbal communication resemble
Hikari's. Dr. Sacks wrote: "Creativity, as usually understood, needs
not only a 'what,' a talent, but a 'who'—strong personal charac-

teristics, a strong identity, personal sensibility, a personal style, which flow into the talent, interfuse it, give it a personal body and form. Creativity in this sense involves the power to originate, to break away from the existing ways of looking at things, to move freely in the realm of the imagination, to create and recreate worlds fully in one's mind—while supervising all this with a critical inner eye. Creativity has to do with inner life, with the flow of new ideas and strong feelings. Creativity, in this sense, will probably never be possible for Stephen." Yet Stephen Wiltshire's pictures, and Hikari's music, indubitably contain something that is communicated from one self to others, something that viewers and listeners have found satisfying and rewarding.

Hikari appears to have trouble in using his reasoning powers to adapt to changing circumstances, though he is obviously not devoid of the ability to reason. He tends to stick to a rigid routine and to get upset if the routine is disrupted. For example, his father has described Hikari's rage when he hustled him across a busy street before the light changed, disrupting the careful procedure Hikari has evolved to minimize the stressfulness of crossing streets. And his mother said he was very distressed by the constant disruptions of the predictable patterns of family life by the onslaught of phone calls and visitors that followed his father's winning the Nobel prize.

Yet even in nonmusical areas, Hikari has demonstrated not only reasoning skills but some imagination and enterprise. For example, having noticed that his father cries when he cuts onions, Hikari, knowing that crying is undesirable and aware that he himself cannot cry, volunteered to cut onions. He has also shown a considerable sense of humor, which is another kind of nonmusical creativity. (Interestingly, his humor has an impish quality, a delight in the subversion of expectations, which is strongly reminiscent of his father's.) When his mother turned fifty-six, in 1992, Hikari's contribution to the birthday card the family made for her read in part: "Happy Birthday. It looks like the number of people turning fifty-six this year is gradually increasing." And one of his most creative jokes actually concerns his creativity itself. When the family was listening to his first CD, he observed, "I have been living for more than thirty years, but my Total Playing Time is just forty-seven minutes, fifty-three seconds." He has used this kind of verbal creativity in some of the more playful titles he has given his pieces, too, such as "May the Plane Not Fall" or "Mister Prelude."

Does creativity require the ability to reason? Many of the psychologists who have studied savantism hope their discoveries will shed light on this question. "Nobody really knows what creativity is," Dr. Treffert said. "Creativity is the ability to produce something new, novel, not simply replicating what you've experienced—*making something new.* Of course, as soon as you've said that, some people will ask, But *is* there anything new under the sun?"

Dr. Bharucha concurs: "The difference between creating and remembering—that's the sixty-four million dollar question! Creativity—it's mysterious, like consciousness; we don't have a good handle on it. We do have strong hints about it, though.

"Creativity consists of putting recognizable building blocks together in new ways. Using features of an established style in such a way that we recognize an individual's stamp on it—this requires judgment. Lots of people try to be creative in ways that other people will appreciate and recognize, but to do that, they need to have judgment about the balance between sticking to established patterns and going beyond them." The success of Hikari's music appears to indicate that this judgment need not necessarily be conscious, or consciously understood.

"One thing we know is that creativity in a particular domain presupposes substantial experience with that domain. So if somebody like Hikari Oe is being creative musically in a particular style, it's almost a certainty that he has had substantial experience with that style. It would be a huge surprise if he were writing pieces that resembled Mozart without having heard quite a bit of Mozart.

"His brain must have included these patterns, and is abstracting some of the regularities that characterize that style. These are the regularities that some people would call 'rules'—chords are followed only by certain other chords, instruments and melodies are used in certain ways, there are typical ways of elaborating on themes. Somebody who has internalized these patterns may be able to use them creatively. This internalization of 'rules' is no guarantee of being able to create, of course, but it is certainly a precondition."

Dr. Miller was intrigued by Hikari's choice of musical idiom. "It sounds to me as though his early exposure was crucial. Even his prenatal exposure; I'm becoming more impressed with recent research on that. And his parents' persistence in speaking to him may have played a role at the same time. There have been some controlled studies in the recent past suggesting that early experience with and exposure to particular musical genres may combine in particular ways with experiences of hearing the human voice. There is something about the structural characteristics of certain kinds of classical music, especially Mozart. It's something about the variation within regularity, you can listen to Mozart forever. There is a beautiful range of variations but they occur within a structure that's relatively tractable. There have been a number of hypotheses about whether it's the regularity of the metric structure or the regularity of tonality, but whatever it is seems to reflect certain aspects of the human voice, and to take advantage of the predilection for the prosodic features of human language. These studies have produced evidence of exposure to music like Mozart's having potent effects on brain development in human infants."

Hikari's tastes certainly do not extend far beyond the eighteenth- and nineteenth-century music he was exposed to in early life. He dislikes most contemporary music, with a few exceptions, such as Takemitsu's early, comparatively simple and conventional works and some of Messiaen's less complicated religious pieces. And Hikari did once imitate Takemitsu's experiments with calligraphic music in a composition in honor of one of his favorite sumo hero's victories, using clusters of notes that represented his hands pushing his opponent out of the ring. He labeled the piece "Modern Music." When Hikari was in the restaurant of the Mayflower Hotel in New York with his father in the fall of 1996, Iannis Xenakis, who recognized Kenzaburo from photographs, came over to their table, introduced himself, and offered his condolences on the death of Takemitsu, knowing he had been a close friend of Kenzaburo's. Hikari is generally polite and usually delighted to meet musical luminaries—especially composers—but although Kenzaburo explained who the man was, Hikari kept his eyes down and said nothing at all. After Xenakis went back to his own table, Kenzaburo asked Hikari why on earth he had been so rude. "I don't like his music," Hikari said. Kenzaburo says that when he himself is listening to contemporary-classical music or jazz, Hikari will tolerate it politely but seems to be waiting for the sound system to be free again so that he can listen to the classical and romantic works he favors.

Large numbers of normal children have had substantial exposure to classical music in early childhood, and some of them retain a preference for it in later life. Hikari actually went on to compose it. One would think that the disadvantages Hikari had to surmount to become a composer—in any idiom—would surely have stifled any but the strongest creative drive. What can explain Hikari's unstoppable creativity?

Kenzaburo's literary achievements show striking creativity; he is not only notably prolific but outstandingly inventive and innovative, and Hikari's maternal grandfather's work has the same qualities. Kenzaburo's creativity manifests itself in trivial ways, too. Psychologists say that compulsive fiddling with objects is an indication of a creative temperament. By this measure, as by all others, Kenzaburo is extraordinarily creative: during one interview, he manipulated a key chain he was holding so energetically that he broke it in two; during another, he fidgeted ceaselessly with a curtain cord. Whether or not specifically musical talents are heritable, most psychologists feel that creativity itself is in some sense a heritable trait. Dr. Bharucha said he wouldn't be surprised if a genetic component was at least partly responsible for Hikari's exceptional creative achievements. "Certainly, there are substantial differences in people's creativity, and it *would* surprise me if environmental differences accounted for it. There are people who have worked on this question, but the literature is disappointing. One theme you encounter again and again in the literature on creativity is that the two necessary conditions are exposure and hard work. But people can have the same amount of exposure and put the same amount of hard work into things, yet some will be creative and others not."

Dr. Treffert does not doubt that creativity is heritable. "Yes, indeed," he said. "But of course, creativity isn't a thing you absolutely have or don't have, it's a spectrum—with some people being more creative and some people being less so. And the tendency for that to be transmitted genetically is certainly there. One inherits a variety of traits, e.g., shyness, or being optimistic or pessimistic—not all one's traits are learned. These are affected by life experiences, but they can be inherited as traits."

Creativity is a conspicuously elusive concept: nobody knows precisely what creativity consists of, and many scientists are wary of committing themselves even to speculations about its nature and origins. But many theories about its possible physical causes have sprung up in recent years. One, plausibly expounded by Dr. Kay Redfield Jamison in her book *Touched with Fire,* sees a strong link between manic-depressive illness (bipolar disorder) and creation. The scientific consensus today on bipolar disorder is that, while it is not heritable in the sense that, say, color blindness may be, the physical factors that make it possible are heritable. In this way it is more like alcoholism; one may inherit traits that put one at risk for developing it, but experiential factors will determine whether it actually develops.

It would be presumptuous and wrongheaded—and, in any case, impossible—to attempt to diagnose Kenzaburo Oe on the basis of fiction he has written about depressive characters, merely because they seem to be understood from the inside, their points of view being represented believably (and movingly). But it is surely permissible to consider this fiction in conjunction with forthright autobiographical statements he has made from time to time—for example, about the slough of despond he fell into at the time of Hikari's birth. Kenzaburo has said he has experienced symptoms of clinical depression, including suicidal thoughts and impulses. And his descriptions of his work habits, and of elations he has experienced—particularly of certains "highs" his relationship with Hikari has given him— suggest that he has a manic side, too. After Takemitsu's death, Kenzaburo spoke of being "haunted" by Takemitsu's "spirit." He was careful to explain that he was speaking metaphorically, yet his account suggested a saner version of Robert Schumann's description of being possessed by the spirit of Schubert (which, in the terms of modern psychiatry, would be classed as a delusional symptom of a manic phase). And Hikari has a history of slipping from time to time into slumps of sullen, withdrawn, and even violent behavior. Evidently, he, too, experiences euphoria from time to time—it is unmistakably apparent when his work is applauded at concerts. Father and son may both have some form of bipolar disorder, and it may be a factor in their inclination—and ability—to create.

Kenzaburo himself sees Hikari's bouts of depression as consequences both of his epileptic seizures and of the drugs he must take to control them. Another theory about the physical causes of creativity, expounded by Eve LaPlante in *Seized* and W. G. and M. A. Lennox in *Epilepsy and Related Disorders,* holds that epilepsy itself may sometimes be involved in the creative process, though. But

Kenzaburo maintains that Hikari's epilepsy has only dampened his creativity and cannot have enhanced it in any way.

Kenzaburo and Yukari obviously played a crucial role in fostering Hikari's creativity, not just genetically but in more direct ways. For one thing, Kenzaburo set an extraordinarily compelling example, sitting in the same room with him, day after day, creating imaginative literature with disciplined and dedicated productivity. And Yukari has been drawing throughout Hikari's life. Imitation of the models his parents provided was surely a factor in Hikari's transcending his limitations in a way no one else has ever done.

The force of example apart, it is clear that Kenzaburo and Yukari's determined, persistent, and imaginative interactions with their speechless infant affected the organic development of his brain—the development that made it possible for him to become a creative artist himself. For the brain continues to grow and develop after a child is born; in fact, experiences during the first three years of life are crucial to the physical organization of the brain. (Stimulation is crucial for nonhuman brains, too; even mice who grow up in a stimulating environment have more brain cells than unstimulated mice.) Findings from recent studies in cognitive neuroscience presented at Hillary Rodham Clinton's conference on early child development in April 1997 emphasized the importance of spoken language in cerebral growth, identifying creativity specifically as a trait that could be promoted by speaking frequently to infants. As Sandra Blakeslee put it in her report on these findings for the *New York Times*, "Some researchers say the number of words an infant hears each day is the single most important predictor of later intelligence." And "the words have to come from an attentive, engaged human being."

It has been known for a long time that stimulation is crucial to the organic growth of the brain: stimulation strengthens neurons, which respond by establishing new synaptic connections. Without stimulation, many brain cells simply die; with it, they thrive. This means that a stimulated infant winds up with many more brain cells than an unstimulated one, and the most effective means of stimulation is animated interaction with a human being. In short, if you want your baby to grow up smart, talk to it, and the more you talk to it, the smarter it will be. The most growth-promoting style of talking to infants is an animated, engaged, affirmative one—a style recognizable at once to anyone who has read Kenzaburo's writing, both factual and fictionalized, about the way he spoke to Hikari when Hikari was a child.

Can creativity itself be deliberately created? Apparently it can, in some ways, and a question like "Did Kenzaburo create Hikari's creativity?" turns out to be far less fanciful than it seems. Kenzaburo's determinedly creative approach to raising Hikari was in a very direct, literal, and physical sense responsible for cultivating Hikari's capacity to create. The more neuronal connections an adult has to draw on, the more intelligent he will be—and the more intelligent he is, in this sense, the more creative potential he will have. Elusive though creativity may be, everyone agrees that creating involves making connections, and the connections the brain has physically made enable it to connect ideas in the course of using them.

Dr. Treffert said the recent studies weren't really new discoveries, only additional confirmations of something already known. "When I wrote my book, I concentrated on the prenatal period, because I thought the research that had already been done at that time was so well known that I didn't need to go into what happened to the brain after a baby is born. The best method for developing brain cells is still a mother—or a father—talking to a child. If the Oes had taken their doctors' advice, or believed them when they said that trying to talk to Hikari was a waste of time, the outcome would have been very different. Without stimulation, cells die. The extent to which synapses are formed has a great deal to do with what neurons are developed and continue to develop, both after and before birth. The Oes' continuing this relentless interaction, speaking to him and trying to teach him to talk had much to do with the outcome for Hikari. In his case, I think we can find proof of the fact that when you have a damaged hemisphere, you can compensate with the remaining hemisphere. The manner in which his talents demonstrated themselves had to do with which parts of the brain were available and intact.

"The phenomenon of keeping synapses linked continues throughout life. Those neurons not activated by synapses developing are probably discarded. Of course, it's most important when the brain is new, and it's particularly important in kids, whose brains are still plastic, malleable. With youngsters—and this is especially true for someone like Hikari—you can take advantage of the brain's malleability while it is there. If his parents had not been interactive with him, a window of opportunity would have been lost. It's like some vitamin deficiencies: if a child is deprived during certain periods of development, conditions may arise which you couldn't correct later on, because it would be too late. You might even have certain irreversible deformities, like the bone deformities you see in rickets as a result of deprivation of vitamin D. With Hikari, this intense interaction was not an elective or optional thing—and if it had been introduced suddenly, at a later point, the opportunity would have been lost forever, it would have been too late, so having a lot of interaction in the first years of life was definitely very critical for him.

"A proclivity to create is certainly heritable. The fact that Hikari Oe had a mental handicap limited what he could do in terms of brain development, but the genes, the traits, were still there. I would say that in addition to his particular brain circuitry, that is what accounts for his being creative compared to other savants, and his environment would reinforce the traits he inherited, his father creating literature, his mother drawing all the time, and so on. In Hikari's case, the circuitry crossover was not absolute, and then there is his genetic background and his experience of a re-

inforcing environment. Because without creative traits and reinforcement for creativity, savants are *not* creative."

While creativity remains a slippery concept, scientists now
feel they understand some of the physical factors that make it possible; by exposing the inadequacies of some previous assumptions
about savant limitations, Hikari's case may be helpful in solving
some of the remaining puzzles. As Dr. Treffert puts it, "Hikari really *is* exceptional, and unique in more than one way. His creativity is extraordinary in itself, but so is the fact that he has actually
shown creativity in more than one area. The titles of his pieces
show verbal creativity. So do the jokes he has made—wit is definitely a form of creativity. And his father's appreciation of his puns
and jokes undoubtedly reinforced this proclivity. Hikari is exceptional not just in the fact of his creating music, but in the creative
use he has made of emotion in his compositions—this is entirely
unlike what other savants have done. I find the greater musical
complexity and emotional depth of the pieces on his second CD
entirely remarkable, the way mood is conveyed by the music in relationship to the style of writing is very remarkable—and it's definitely *there* in the music, not just something we'd like to imagine
about it."

Yet artistic creation itself is ultimately mysterious, and while
Hikari is a "case," he is also an artist. Even Dr. Sacks, after discussing past and present scientific theories (including his own),
warns his readers against imagining that such theories can "explain" what must, in the end, remain a mystery: "Although the interpretation of the lives and works and personalities of eminent
figures in terms of their supposed neurological or psychiatric dis-
positions is not new, it has become an obsession, almost an industry, at the present time. . . . Books and articles attribute Tourette's
syndrome to Samuel Johnson and Mozart, autism to Bartók and
Einstein, and manic-depressive illness to virtually every creative
artist. . . . It may well be that many of these attributions are correct. The danger is that we may go overboard in medicalizing our

predecessors (and contemporaries), reducing their complexity to expressions of neurological or psychiatric disorder, while neglecting all the other factors that determine a life, not least the irreducible uniqueness of the individual." Hikari is exceptional among savants as a composer, and exceptional among composers as a savant. But he is also exceptional in a different, less taxonomic way: the way all artists are exceptional, working within the rules of their various art forms to offer us their own irreplaceably particular visions and voices.

Somersaults

In a lecture given at a concert of Hikari's music, Kenzaburo said that one of the basic needs of a creative artist is the development of his art, noting that his own progress as a writer had reflected this need. But when he came to America in September 1996, the need had gone unfulfilled for two years, ever since Hikari's success had prompted him to renounce writing fiction. He had said that for about thirty years, his primary motivation in writing fiction had been the need to speak for Hikari, who could not speak for himself. Now Hikari had found a way to make his own voice heard. "Besides, I have been writing for almost forty years now, and I thought I had worked enough and earned a rest."

Kenzaburo came to teach at Princeton University for a year, hoping to enjoy a respite from the consequences of his fame in Japan. Planning no more creative labor, he intended to spend the year studying Spinoza; his teaching duties would be light. And he would be living alone, in a sparsely furnished faculty apartment in a nondescript modern building near the campus, although Yukari and Hikari would be joining him there for a few weeks in November for concerts of Hikari's music and readings to promote *A Healing Family*. It was a modest apartment but had a spectacular view of Carnegie Lake. Kenzaburo had brought very few things there; one was a bath mat with a picture of Winnie the Pooh to remind him of his absent son.

He said that in Japan, after Hikari became such a successful composer and he himself won the Nobel, they were beleaguered by fans and well-wishers whenever they left the house. Taking Hikari to and from the welfare workplace in the past, Kenzaburo would use the time constructively: reading, studying, or just thinking about whatever he was writing. But that had become impossible, with strangers greeting him and Hikari wherever they went, often asking for autographs or wanting to talk to them. Hikari enjoyed the friendly attention, but Kenzaburo sorely missed the opportunity to pursue his thoughts in peace. He found tranquillity in Princeton. When he arrived, it was particularly quiet there: the campus was nearly deserted; classes had not yet begun.

Within a few days, he began a new novel, renouncing his renunciation. In fact, he had not so much renounced it as modified it. Since it had been Hikari's success that prompted him to abandon fiction, he realized he didn't need to give up writing fiction altogether, but he was going to give up writing fiction about Hikari.

Once again, it was a voiceless composer who inspired him to write. In this case, the composer was Toru Takemitsu, one of his oldest and closest friends, whose death in February of that year had been a devastating loss. "I had been to visit him in the hospital. And when we talked about my decision to give up writing fiction, he didn't condemn it directly, but he gave me a very peculiar smile—sad and a little bit malicious. I spoke at his funeral, and they played some music he had written called 'Rain Tree,' inspired by stories of mine. I kept thinking of that smile and what it meant. When I first came to Princeton, I was going from my office to my apartment, and there are three rain trees on the way. So I sat down under one of them, and I saw that smile of Takemitsu's, like the Cheshire Cat's. And I knew that the only way I could stand up before his spirit was to write novels again."

The return to writing fiction—doing what he does best—had obviously made him happy. He was also rejoicing because he had recently learned that some ear trouble Hikari had been having, which had worried his family horribly since listening is so essential for him, was only external and easy to cure. Kenzaburo's famously mischievous grin flashed frequently as he spoke about it, and he seemed positively gleeful as he described the book he had just begun.

He said that some of its themes would echo previous works, and that he expected it to be his longest by far. He had put down his pen in the middle of a homosexual seduction scene. "So, I have left my characters at a very critical moment," he said. "There is an artist, a man in his sixties—he is famous for developing arts education in Japan, but he is teaching at an American university—and he is about to have an affair with a young terrorist who belongs to a religious cult, something like Aum Shinrikyo [the cult that released poison gas into the Tokyo subway]. The artist is painting a picture of Jonah, the Old Testament character, using this terrorist as a model, and he is looking at his beautiful young body and wondering how he is going to proceed.

"I already have the title. It will be called 'Somersault.' I got the idea while reading about a man called Shabbetai Tzevi, who proclaimed himself a Messiah and was arrested in Constantinople in the seventeenth century. You know, many people expected a Messiah in 1666. The Ottomans arrested Tzevi, and he apostatized instantly— converted from Judaism to Islam, wore a turban and all. But some of his followers continued to believe he was the Messiah and decided that his apostasy must somehow be part of his mission."

Asked how he felt about his own somersault, he said, "I was listening to Bach's B-Minor Mass," he said, "and thinking of Takemitsu's spirit, that his spirit had become part of the cosmos now, of some cosmic spirit that I could hear in the Bach." To make sure it was understood he was not talking literally about some ghostly visitation, Kenzaburo explained that he is neither superstitious nor conventionally religious, and does not believe in the supernatural. "But I felt that this cosmic spirit of Takemitsu approved of what I am doing," he said.

Consistently, Kenzaburo appears to need to believe he is speaking for others, or somehow fulfilling the wishes of their spirits, when he writes. Of course, all writers need to believe something of the kind, but it seems unusually concrete in his case. Perhaps he had become so accustomed to thinking of himself as the only conduit for Hikari's voice in the world that, once Hikari found a way to speak directly to the public, Kenzaburo required a substitute to legitimize his own need for creative expression.

Yet, while there are many indications in his work that he is troubled by the selfish choices that the life of an artist may entail, he is also aware that art is healing—initially for the artist and ultimately for the audience that enjoys his works. "In the music or literature we create," he wrote, "we come to know despair . . . we find that by actually giving it expression we can be healed and know the joy of recovering: and as these linked experiences of pain and recovering are added to one another, layer upon layer, not only is the artist's work enriched but its benefits are shared with others."

Even so, Kenzaburo's continuing sense of guilt is distressingly apparent, both in his writings and when he speaks in person. It seems gratuitous. He has been a singularly responsible and dedicated parent. His public life has been admirably responsible, too; he has been extremely generous with his time, talents, and energy in the service of the causes he holds dear, supporting nuclear disarmament, denouncing discrimination against ethnic minorities in Japan, protesting the persecution of dissident writers in repressive Asian regimes, and, of course, tirelessly pressing for the full integration of the disabled into Japanese society. Yet he seems to feel that he has done less than his duty.

In a particularly startling passage in *A Healing Family,* he recounts his reactions on being sent some pages from a journal by the doctor who performed the operation that saved Hikari's life. It sheds light on the almost obsessive worrying over the writer-father's guilt in *A Quiet Life.* Kenzaburo was horrified to read that he had hesitated to authorize that operation. Given that *A Personal Matter,* written more than thirty years ago and still his most famous work, could be summed up as a long account of a young father's hesitation about authorizing the same operation on an infant with the same condition, one would think its author would have grown used to the knowledge that he had hesitated to make the same decision. Yet he writes of the doctor's words as "reminding me yet again that if there is a god, some higher being who judges us, then when my time comes I will be unable to face this being with a clear conscience, condemned in advance by this one piece of evidence alone." One wonders if the thing Kenzaburo—one of the most imaginative writers of our time—cannot forgive himself is the lack of imagination involved in his failure to foresee that a "monster baby" would, as he has often written elsewhere that Hikari did, save his life, and that his birth, a seeming disaster at the time, has proven to be an extraordinary blessing that strengthened his family immeasurably, in part through forcing them all to use their imaginations for one another's benefit in dealing with Hikari's needs.

Some of Kenzaburo's guilt may reflect his awareness of some resentment from his daughter, whose determination not to be involved in publicity about the family suggests that she still suffers from the effects of her father's exposures of their family life. And some of it may reflect an unease about whether his attention to Hikari's needs has short-shrifted both her and Sakurao. After having given up so much time to escort Hikari to Karasuyama every day for years, Sakurao, while rejoicing in Hikari's success and loyally prepared to defend him against his critics, does not enjoy a close relationship with his brother today. He no longer lives at home but stays in a worker's dormitory in Chiba, not far to the east of Tokyo, near his company's research center.

"Comparing my brother's life when he was young to his life now that he's grown up, I think the biggest change is that fact that he is now able to work in a vocational center," Sakurao said. "As far as I can see, he seems to have found something to enjoy in the work he does there. But, because of his health, and the need for someone to escort him to and from the workplace, it is unclear how long he will be able to continue this work. I think it is really wonderful that he has been recognized as a composer. It is great that the CD sold, but what's even better—and this is because of the fact that it got so popular—is that he was able to take in the impressions of others, because so many people listened to his music. On top of that, I think that it was especially wonderful for him to have excellent musicians playing his music. However, I feel that there are a lot of people who do not want to give my brother credit for his talent and hard work; they consider his success as a composer to be the result of shrewd management by my family— that kind of thing. There are a number of people in my circle of acquaintances who say this, too. Although I do not know anything about music, I feel that they are only expressing their own dissatisfactions. At present, I think that relations between my brother and me are not as rosy as many people around the world might suppose from my father's writings. I do not praise my brother excessively, and I never go out of my way to communicate with him. Nevertheless, I think I would probably react by being protective of him when people evaluate him narrowly or are critical of the creative efforts he has undertaken. This is hardly an exciting scenario, but I think my relationship with my brother will probably continue along these lines."* But Kenzaburo says that, while Hikari relies on Natsumiko, he considers Sakurao "the champion of our family."

Natsumiko and Sakurao did not accompany Yukari and Hikari when they came to stay with Kenzaburo in Princeton. The whole family had been briefly reunited; Kenzaburo went back to Japan to help his wife cope with the difficulties of making a long trip with Hikari, including taking him to medical appointments to see whether he was up to it. Hikari had also taken it upon himself to prepare for coming to America by imitating a Japanese standup comedian called Toni Tani, whose routines develop around a kind of invented language that's partly English, partly Japanese, and partly pure nonsense. His mother says his imitations are perfect; one is reminded of Oliver Sacks' description of the savant artist Stephen Wiltshire's imitations of the sound of Japanese after a brief trip to Japan. Hikari had wanted to try speaking this nonsense language to the audiences at his concerts—it always gets lots of laughs at home. "But we told him, people will be moved by your music, don't spoil it," Kenzaburo said.

Just before they left for America, they went to visit Yukari's mother, Kimi Ikeuchi. She had lived with them in Tokyo off and on over a twelve-year period and always had a very good relationship with Hikari. Now ninety-three, she needed full-time care and lived in an old people's home just one train station away from the Oes. They usually visited her there every few days. On that last visit, Yukari said, "We were wondering if she would still recognize us.

*Translation by Anita Keire.

She did, and"—reproachful old ladies being much the same all over the world—"she said, 'So, you're still alive.'" Family obligations fulfilled, Kenzaburo, Yukari, and Hikari flew to New York.

For twenty-four hours after arriving in America, Hikari didn't speak at all, and his mother and father were worried about him. But on his second day in the country, as the family was taking a walk by the lake outside their apartment, a flock of Canada geese passed overheard, and Hikari, listening to their cries, called out, "E flat!" and they knew he was all right. As soon as he got back to the apartment, he began working on a new piece, called "Canada Geese"—in E-flat major, of course. (Kenzaburo said later that Hikari had taken to correcting "ill-educated geese who were chirping off-key.") And Hikari was in excellent spirits for the concert of his music on the campus that night, which was sold out.

When the three of them arrived in the hall, Kenzaburo and Hikari were beseiged by fans wanting autographs on their programs and on books of Kenzaburo's that they had brought. In person, the Oes are a stunning family. Kenzaburo's impish charm and dapper turnouts must have been familiar to many in the audience from his frequent television appearances. Some might have seen Yukari and Hikari in the NHK documentary about their family life, which shows them mostly in a deliberately everyday light and gives no hint of how glamorous they can be.

Hikari is handsome. The documentary never shows him in repose. In motion or conversation, his jerky movements and sometimes strange or lost-looking expressions are so striking that they prevent one from noticing how attractive his features are, how well-built he is, and what a smooth, glowing complexion he has. Kenzaburo has written about having developed the habit of looking in on Hikari at night to see whether he was all right or needed anything, and often being amazed by the beauty of his sleeping son, which he didn't usually notice when Hikari was awake because he had to worry constantly about him or address his immediate problems.

On this occasion the Oes all looked elegant, too. Yukari was a polished, worldly beauty, a contrast to most of the women in the suburban and academic audience. Her hair, worn shoulder-length, was sleek; so was her black pantsuit, worn with a red bow-collar silk blouse and fashionably chunky shoes. Her hands, with red-lacquered nails, looked newly manicured. Surely she was tired; she had come from Japan only the day before, yet there was no trace of weariness about her. She was born in 1936, but she looked about forty that night.

Kenzaburo studied the text of his preconcert speech intently, perhaps to discourage autograph seekers. His dark suit and white shirt looked as pristine as if they had both been bought that afternoon. He has the slightly irritating quality of always looking dazzlingly well groomed no matter how informally he is dressed. In one interview that fall, his brand-new-looking white running shoes remained perfectly white as we trudged around the muddy campus in the rain, taking wrong turns looking for his new office. Mitigatingly, his hair seems to have a life of its own and is often the sole exception to his disconcerting perpetual tidiness; he ruffled it a little in front as he scrutinized his speech.

When a young man asked Hikari to autograph his program, kneeling down in front of him, Kenzaburo looked up from his sheaf of papers and leaned over his son to supervise this operation, protecting and guiding. Hikari signed the program very carefully and deliberately. His father says that Hikari is often asked for autographs now, but he plainly hasn't become used to giving them.

Hikari sat quietly looking very dignified, if a bit stiff and confused. (His body movements are awkward, but he has remarkably graceful hands, small, delicate, and beautifully shaped, with long, tapering fingers.) He wore a dark blue suit with a mandarin-collar jacket, a style similar to a male Japanese high-school student's uniform; his outfit seemed generically Asian and vaguely futuristic. His glasses have extremely thick lenses, testifying to the severity of his visual impairment. His shoes were black, shapeless, and orthopedic-looking; his socks were brown. The plastic plate in his head is conspicuous from the back; no attempt has been made to cover it with his hair. Much has been written about his difficulty in conveying emotions, but as he talked to his parents, the expressiveness and mobility of his face were striking.

When Kenzaburo took the stage, he told the audience about Hikari's reaction to the Canada geese. (Hikari laughed, happy at recognizing the title of his piece among the unfamiliar English words.) His speech continued with an account of how, almost ten years before, a doctor at Tokyo University Hospital had asked him, in the course of one of Hikari's medical examinations, "What is your vocation?" And Kenzaburo was shocked, because he thought he was well known. But then the doctor asked whether he was an interpreter for handicapped children, because he interpreted so well for Hikari. Kenzaburo thought at the time that such a vocation would be more important than that of a novelist. Later, he realized that a novelist *is* an interpreter, listening to the inner voices of people who have no method of expressing themselves; the novelist must listen to the fragmentary expressions of such people and create to reveal the meanings hidden in their hearts.

He had felt that he must do this with his son's heart. He wanted to listen to the way Hikari expressed himself, whether in words or in silence, and use what he discovered to express a universal voice of humanity, especially suffering humanity, and create hope for everyone through the voice he created for his son.

But an odd reversal happened when his son began composing. What Kenzaburo heard in Hikari's music was *his own inner voice,* a voice that was at the same time almost transcendental, a truly human voice, the voice of someone who had experienced suffering. "Now," he said, "I wonder how my son developed as an interpreter of *my* soul through the language of music." He said that new mishaps occur almost every year in his family and new challenges to conquer; the important thing, throughout their vicissitudes, has been that all the members of his family have healed themselves and one another, and he concluded by reading from his essay about how pain is transmuted to joy through the act of creation.

Hiroshi Koizumi had come from Japan with Hiroyuki Okano, who took vacation time and came at his own expense, for this and another concert of Hikari's music. They stayed in Princeton with the Oes. ("But we were so busy while they were here that we didn't so much as give them a cup of tea," Yukari said.) The instrumentalists who joined Mr. Koizumi for the Princeton concert were both Japanese: the pianist Chie Sato Roden, a specialist in contemporary repertory who plays American composers in Japan and Japanese composers in America, and the violinist Mayuki Fukuhara, who began his career as a child prodigy and is now a member of the St. Luke's Chamber Ensemble and of Orpheus.

Hikari listened intently as they played, often with his chin propped on his left hand, tapping out rhythms there with his fingers, then wrapping them around his jaw. Noticing a fluffed note in the solo-piano "Barcarole," he frowned. Soon there was another fluff, but this time he smiled, forgivingly. In "Nocturnal Capriccio," which plainly went over very well with the audience, Mr. Fukuhara used greater dynamic variation and more exaggerated tempos than those of Tomoko Kato on the second CD. Hikari raised his eyebrows, seeming surprised by this new interpretation. Asked after the concert which player he had liked best, he unhesitatingly named Mr. Koizumi—who, after all, is not only a friend but the player Hikari has always had in mind when writing for the flute.

As Hikari took his bows after the concert, his delight was evident. It was even more apparent later, as he stood in the lobby to receive congratulations, flanked by two of his father's students who had volunteered to interpret for him and take care of him in case of trouble. He was beaming, radiant, unmistakably elated. In an essay, his father described seeing Hikari for a moment on the local television news after a concert in Shikoku that included his music: "the young composer, receiving a bouquet, the picture of joy and excitement." He presented the same picture that night.

There were two more performances of Hikari's music in America while he was here, both in New York, at the Japan Society, on Friday, November 15, with Hiroshi Koizumi, Ken Noda, and Cho-Liang Lin. One, in the afternoon, was really an open rehearsal; local schoolchildren had been invited. The Japan Society had originally planned it as a concert for children from schools for the mentally disabled, but there had been logistical difficulties, so the audience was mixed, with most of the children coming from ordinary schools. Their behavior testified to the appeal of Hikari's music; they listened with such quiet, rapt attention that it was actually possible to forget one was surrounded by schoolchildren. They made no noise at all until the concert was over, when they burst into prolonged, noisy applause.

The evening concert was a more formal event than the afternoon performance. A Japanese television crew was filming the arrivals as the New York Japanese-studies community turned out in full force. The lobby was packed. The tickets (nearly three hundred) had sold out soon after they went on sale, and the full theater made it evident that the unseasonably severe cold hadn't kept anyone at home.

Kenzaburo introduced the concert with a speech nearly identical to the one he had delivered in Princeton. The instrumentalists' performances were similar to those they had given in the afternoon, but, predictably, there was more tension and energy in the air. Afterward, there was a reception for the Oes and the players. Kenzaburo and Yukari were mobbed. At first, while standing with them to receive congratulations, Hikari seemed as elated as he had been after the Princeton concert. Most of the guests were bilingual, but whenever Hikari wandered away from his parents, he was strikingly neglected. Plainly, Hikari's well-publicized difficulties in communicating have a discouraging effect. The high of the concert was visibly wearing off. He seemed a little lost, and weary, but his expression was characteristically patient.

Asked what he thought of the performance that night, Hikari only smiled enigmatically. Mr. Noda's playing had been strikingly beautiful: precise, delicate, full of sensitivity and variety of expression, his experience as a lieder accompanist (he has accompanied Hildegard Behrens and Maria Ewing) evident as he followed the flute. Consistently flawless and consistently exquisite, savoring every nuance, he had brought out expressive subtleties in Hikari's music that Ms. Ebi's performances on the CDs had not revealed. But no matter what he was asked about Mr. Noda's interpretation or how the question was rephrased, Hikari had nothing to say about it. Mr. Lin was eager to know what Hikari had thought of his own performance, but Hikari's replies, after the question was put in several different ways, were determinedly evasive. One got the impression that he was being tactful.

But when asked, "Yummy, huh?" while he was unself-consciously wolfing down hors d'oeuvres, he unhesitatingly answered, "Delicious," flashing a charming, boyish grin. It is very difficult to tell how he is feeling at any given moment, and his father has exploited both the comic and the pathetic potentials of this uncertainty in his writing about Hikari and characters based on him. But his pleasure in food is evident, unself-conscious, and entirely unambiguous, like a teenage boy's. His mother said that he eats everything; he is the only one in the family who has no food dislikes.

Asked how he liked America, Hikari replied, "It's fine," but it was impossible to draw him out on the subject. His mother said he seemed to like it and that he settled down into his old listening routines as soon as he found the classical station on the radio. "At home, the phone is always ringing, or people are coming to the door, there are always lots of new people he doesn't know coming to visit or call on the family. And he can always tell when I'm irritated by having to deal with so many people, and it makes him very nervous. But he doesn't have that kind of thing to cope with here, and he seems more relaxed in this peaceful place." Although he doesn't like constant intrusions, she confirmed what Kenzaburo had said about Hikari's enjoying some aspects of his fame and getting a real kick out of being recognized by strangers. "There was a lot of publicity about him because of the first CD, and even when we went to Hokkaido people would call out to him by name on the street, and he was absolutely delighted. But it was the TV program that made him really well known. When we go out now, we know what it's like to be a television personality." She sighed, eloquently. "My husband finds it a real nuisance. Hikari mostly likes it, though."

In Princeton, the Oes mostly stayed home together all day when they had nothing scheduled. They had no car (they have none in Japan). Neither Kenzaburo nor Yukari drives, though she has a license. This is nowhere near as unusual for Japanese in their circumstances as it would be for Americans. Kenzaburo once said that officious people suggest from time to time that they should get a car for Hikari's sake, just in case they need fast transportation in a medical emergency, "but it's never the doctors who say that." In Princeton by himself, Kenzaburo set forth on foot or on his bicycle to buy groceries, and generally cooked his own meals. When Yukari and Hikari were there, Yukari usually went shopping with the wife of another Japanese professor who had a car, and the Oes hired cars with drivers for their family excursions. Hikari and Yukari stayed in Princeton for about three weeks. "It was wonderful," Kenzaburo said later. "Just like Japan—only more peaceful. We are not so famous here, so nobody disturbed us."

Hikari missed Natsumiko, though. They kept in touch by fax nearly every day, and he waited impatiently for her faxes: "He really leans on her," his mother said. He also counted on fax communication to keep him apprised of the latest sumo scores. He sent Natsumiko charmingly illustrated letters that looked like the work of a very clever child. One showed a waiter at the Rihga Royal Hotel (where the Oes stayed in New York), poised with a dessert cart over the Oes' table; Hikari depicted the scene because—as he explained in the text—the waiter had prefaced his recital of the names of the desserts with "ladies and gentlemen," which is how Toni Tani begins his routines. Another, depicting a man lowering himself into a bathtub, was captioned "Coming to New York." This was one of Hikari's puns—the words in Japanese sound like "entering hot water."

Natsumiko takes Hikari out on Sundays. They go to a coffee shop then shop for CDs, books, and magazines. Besides the FM listings in the newspaper that enable him to plan his classical-listening schedule—an important ritual for him—he buys classical-music magazines, which he devours, especially enjoying background articles about upcoming broadcasts, so that he can listen in a well-informed way. And as a big fan of sumo wrestling, he buys all the magazines devoted to that sport to keep up with his favorite stars. His involvement with it is intense; he never misses a sumo broadcast on television, even when this rules out some other pleasure, like an outing with his sister. His mother said that he really looks forward to their excursions; she thinks they're the high point of his week. But at sumo tournament time, even music takes a back seat, and his emotional engagement in the contests becomes so extreme that he has been known to have seizures when one of his favorite wrestlers suffers a reversal.

But neither being with his sister nor being where he can get up-to-the-minute sumo information can keep Hikari on an even keel when he is separated from his father for long periods of time. In December, when he had been back in Tokyo without Kenzaburo for nearly a month, he had some sort of depressive crisis. He had been cheerful enough for the first three months while his father was teaching at Princeton, and mostly very happy when the family was reunited there. But following his pattern, as Kenzaburo's absence dragged on, he became increasingly unhappy and difficult to get along with.

The crisis came at a particularly bad time for Kenzaburo, who was preparing to leave for Mexico City, where he had agreed to deliver a lecture in January. "My wife was very deeply troubled," Kenzaburo said. "She told me Hikari was entirely against her and the other members of the family, and she didn't know how to cope. He resisted everything, wouldn't speak, wouldn't eat. My wife felt unable to handle him by herself, and asked me to try rescuing her by talking to Hikari on the phone. At first, he refused to come to the phone when she told him I wanted to speak to him. But I continued calling, frequently, and always asked her to try again to make him talk to me. Finally he agreed to take the phone, and his voice was very dark, very melancholy. I spoke to him for thirty or forty minutes, but he didn't say much. After that, I sent him many faxes—for two or three days, I sent ten or twenty every day. I told him he had to cooperate with his mother and sister—if he didn't, how could they live on? After three days of this, his mind changed, and when I spoke to him, his voice gradually became very quiet and very polite, and when I asked if he would cooperate with them, he said, 'Yes.' My wife phoned me soon after that, and she was actually laughing with relief, saying I had rescued her. She said he had changed so much that he even looked like a different person, that he was now very polite and good. I continued to send him faxes almost every day, as long as he seemed to need it. It's four months later now, and I'm faxing him about once a week these days, to prevent a relapse. My wife says he's sometimes very melancholy and not very cordial but nothing like before. And that was the only time he got very bad since I came to Princeton."

Reflecting on his son's behavior, Kenzaburo said, "Hikari is thirty-four now, he's a middle-aged man. And in his long life, he has become melancholy in the past ten years. Until he turned twenty, he was usually very gay and merry, but he has become rather melancholic and dark and brooding as an adult. We look back now and remember our brighter days, when we were all young and always laughing. Even now, he hasn't lost his sense of humor, though. He still sometimes makes puns and plays on words—I think he enjoys them because he is so sensitive to sounds—and he makes other kinds of jokes, though not as frequently as he used to.

"Every year, on Hikari's birthday, we give a musical party. No one is invited except instrumentalists, who come to play Hikari's music. In the beginning, those parties made him so happy, he was always laughing and speaking excitedly and enjoying himself so much, but in the last three or four years he just listens quietly to the music. I think he is still enjoying himself, but in a silent way. Becoming thirty was a big thing for him, and especially after his CDs came out he became much quieter.

"But I think this started with his epileptic seizures. Before they came on, he was very merry, always laughing—he was a very comforting person then. We can really hear the difference in tape recordings we have of our children speaking in those days. The pills he has to take for the seizures are depressants, and it was after he began taking them that his personality changed."

Hikari's epilepsy has made life darker for the Oe family in many ways. The phenomenon is depressing and terrifying in itself, apart from the side effects of the drugs Hikari must take to control it. Seizures leave him drained, exhausted, frightened, depressed, and ill, and a seizure in a dangerous situation could end his life. The responsibility is a heavy one for family members escorting him outside the home. Some situations—crossing the street, for example—present special dangers, but his body must be supported wherever he is so that he doesn't injure himself through a fall. That's a tiring and nerve-racking job, especially for the two women who must often do it. Hikari is quite big. His mother is sixty-one, neither large nor strong, and his sister is petite and not at all athletic. The incontinence that accompanies the seizures is, of course, a terrible nuisance, too.

Just keeping him supplied with antiseizure medications is a major chore. Ever since he was fifteen, someone from the family has had to go to a university hospital to collect these drugs once a month, and the trip there and back again takes the better part of a day. Besides that, Hikari needs extensive medical tests, which Kenzaburo has described as "a tiring and sometimes painful ordeal," twice every year to monitor his condition. Sometimes, when his seizures are particularly severe or frequent, he needs extra examinations as well.

Kenzaburo has written about Hikari's epilepsy in a collection of essays called *Loose-Bound Ties,* a follow-up to *A Healing Family,* containing further reflections on the nature of the still-evolving relationships among himself, Yukari, Hikari, Natsumiko, and Sakurao. He discusses the tension between the necessary interdependence of the family members, the natural wish of his two younger children for independent lives, and Hikari's necessary dependence. The title refers to the fact that the ties between them are permanent and real, even if in some cases looser than they used to be. And he expresses his worry, as he has in other writings, about what will become of his wife and children, especially Hikari, after he himself is dead.

In the course of his reflections, he recalls a time when Hikari had what the family calls a "medium-degree" seizure on the way from the train to the welfare workplace when he was escorting him. The incontinence that followed the seizure made it impossible to take a taxi home again because of the smell, so father and son proceeded to Karasuyama. Since Hikari was still "wobbly," Kenzaburo tried to support his body, tried to put his arm around Hikari's shoulders, or simply take his arm, but Hikari wouldn't let him.

When they reached the center, an instructor handed Kenzaburo a change of underwear for Hikari. Kenzaburo was so flustered that he took Hikari into a Japanese-style toilet. Although sometimes quite luxurious, Japanese toilets are basically just holes in the floor, with nothing to sit on. Hikari is not used to using them and in any case was unable to squat. Kenzaburo was reminded of Natsumiko's telling him about coping with Hikari in similar circumstances once, when she was still in high school, trying to support Hikari's body with her own much smaller one in a public toilet in a train station. She had said that the passengers who came in were polite, respectful of Hikari's suffering and her difficulties, and Kenzaburo reflects on what a brave and determined girl she has always been.

On the train going home, Kenzaburo brooded on why Hikari might have refused to let him take his arm on their way to the center and decided that it could only have been because he was feeling so physically sick after his seizure, and that the way he usually accepts his father's help is actually a form of courtesy, which, being a naturally polite person, he would only neglect to show when very sick. Then, as Kenzaburo got off the train, he heard one college girl say to another, in a voice that was purposefully loud enough to reach him, "Did you smell that old man? What a weirdo!"

Kenzaburo concluded that he might have prevented Hikari from becoming more independent by encouraging his patient tolerance of his father's need to feel that he is helping him. He had once lectured at a support group for people with handicapped dependents, and a radical who taught courses in special education had criticized him during the question period that followed by saying that a parent like him was "the archenemy of a child's self-reliance," going on to condemn Kenzaburo's "reactionary" endorsement of "the family," an institution he found politically unacceptable.

His words caused Kenzaburo to ponder his own inability to be independent of Hikari. "Every day, Hikari and I work in the same room, doing our own things, listening to the same music. With a light heart, I go to pick him up at the welfare workshop, and on the way home I incessantly talk to him, as if to piece together the hours we were apart. This has been our daily routine, and somewhere along the line Hikari came to need me, began to think that without me there wouldn't be a decent life for him. Though he never clearly verbalized it, such thoughts had imperceptibly jelled within him. And Hikari endured those thoughts with his will-power, and at the same time tolerated me. This is what dawned on me."

Acutely conscious of his own dependence on Hikari, Kenzaburo has always worried about the implications of Hikari's dependence on him—a worry that grows more acute as Kenzaburo grows older. "I am very anxious about Hikari's future after my death," he says. "Worse, after my wife and I are both dead. We are about to have a very big change in our family now. Natsumiko is going to get married. She is always thinking of her brother. I don't want her to have to make huge sacrifices for him. I hope she can have an independent life with her husband, while still helping us sometimes.

"I think Hikari is sad that he can't have a family of his own. It would be a very good thing if my other children have children, but of course it would make problems, too. But we have always found a new solution for each problem as it arises, so I'm optimistic." After graduating, Natsumiko had a job in the library at her alma mater. "But she has quit her job and is at home all the time now. She takes Hikari to a coffee shop every day. There's a new one near us now in Seijo Gakuen that sells scones. Hikari adores scones, so he's very happy about going there every day with his sister. She will spend a few months this way before her marriage. And after she marries, she will live nearby—we already have an apartment for her—and I will give her a part-time job as a secretary, helping with my literary work. And of course she will be helping with Hikari as well. This is great for my wife. She can get on with her painting while Natsumiko takes over some of her responsibilities. Hikari doesn't have a correct image of his sister's marriage; he can't really understand what it will mean. We must all face a new reality now."

Kenzaburo feels that music will provide continuity for Hikari through any changes he experiences. "Music always makes him happy. And he still creates very merry music sometimes, though recently his music has become sadder—sadder and older, like Hikari himself. I have written, in *A Healing Family,* about how his grief has made it possible for him to write more complicated compositions. But he loves everything about music—reading scores, listening, speaking to musicians. He has true friends through music. There are people he likes from the vocational center. They're friends in a way, but they don't talk to each other. There's someone there I know Hikari thinks is a good man but they don't speak very much. And there is a lot of turnover in the staff; the teachers are always changing at that place. Sometimes he develops close feelings for one teacher, but there are some teachers he just doesn't care about at all. We never interfere in anything that goes on there; we don't want him treated as a special case. And he can enjoy music with people there, too. He plays the accordion there, very skillfully—and bongo drums. His problems with movement don't interfere with that—he's really good.

"I think the musicians he knows are his real friends; they can share something genuine together. I think when musicians visit us, it's the happiest time for Hikari, especially when they are planning to record his music. He talks to them, he answers their questions, and then he creates new music. He's very engaged, and he criticizes what's going on very freely.

"And the way he listens to music every day, concentrating intensely, is a kind of happiness for him. Bach, Beethoven, Chopin, and Mozart have always been his favorites, and he's come to be fonder and fonder of Schubert in the last two years. But he listens to many others, too—Verdi, Telemann. The only modern composer he listens to often is Debussy.

"He is happy when he is scouring the classical-radio program listings to plan his listening schedule or reading classical-music magazines. He has been keeping a diary since he was a child, writing down every piece of music he has listened to every day, and everything he composes, and he still keeps that diary now. He has a music encyclopedia, too—we have a very big one, in Japan—and he reads it all the time. He cannot follow movies, but he will watch musical programs on television besides the ones he hears on the radio. When Hikari is composing music, I think he feels very free—liberated. And he knows huge amounts of music, and I believe the music he knows makes him happy.

"Music makes us all happy, too, in many different ways. Hikari's music has made a big difference in the way people treat my wife. She used to suffer a lot, as the mother of a handicapped boy. But now she is respected as the mother of a composer. No one wants to hear about a disabled person in Japan, but everyone is interested in a composer, and we don't have to protect him from people's prejudices as much as we used to. Yes, I think without music, my family couldn't live on."

Through the recent changes in his life, Hikari has been working on pieces for his next CD, which will be called *The New Hikari Oe.* "I told my son I thought that would be a good title," Kenzaburo says. "Hikari is always very conscientious, and he feels that this title gives him the responsibility of creating something genuinely new." This third recording will include a cello piece and a string quartet. Kenzaburo says the quartet will need a lot of work, but it will be completed for the new recording, and that the three minutes Hikari has already written are very beautiful. "My dream is that he will one day write a real symphony. I would give anything to hear his work played by a full orchestra. I would do anything I had to, to make that happen—even write crime stories, anything!"

Hikari has a new music teacher now, Miss Kabasawa. She is a composer herself and comes once a week to teach him composition. "She is a skillful pianist," Kenzaburo said, "and can play his scores very swiftly. We found her through Hiroshi Koizumi—he knows everybody, he's really the godfather of modern classical music in Japan now. She graduated from a very prestigious school, and has a complete musical education. Ms. Tamura could teach Hikari the fundamental techniques of piano and help him with composing in the beginning, but she had no special knowledge of theory, so finding him a new teacher was really essential at this point."

In May 1997, Kenzaburo, always delighted to report that he has been somehow overtaken by his son, talked about a concert he attended at Carnegie Hall the previous evening. Seiji Ozwa was conducting and invited him to hear Mstislav Rostropovich. When Kenzaburo went backstage to greet Mr. Ozawa, Mr. Rostropovich just acknowledged him politely at first, but when the conductor reminded the cellist that this was the father of Hikari Oe, "He hugged and kissed me!"

He was eight months into his new novel by then. Despite interruptions—a recurrence of his gout and a trip to Spain—he had made good progress, writing at the rate of about ten manuscript pages a day (the equivalent of three in print), and had completed 1,800 first-draft pages of a planned 2,500 (which is to say, the published book will be about 1,200 pages long). He said, "I have wanted to be free from Hikari's influence ever since his music was published. The novel I am writing now will be completely free from Hikari, and in the future I think my writing will be independent of my son." But Hikari is such a big part of Kenzaburo—and has been so important in his writing for so long—that his influence is not so easy to shake. "I say the novel I am writing today is completely free from Hikari, but in fact the part I am working on now has a character who is very close to Hikari. When I think about a very innocent spirit, I want to write episodes about Hikari. So even when I want or try to cut him off, he appears in my draft, and sometimes I find I am quoting things Hikari has actually said. The false-messiah character is very innocent. He is a complicated person, too, but in his innocence he does resemble my son. I find myself giving him Hikari's voice sometimes. That will be an important part of my job when I do the next draft—getting Hikari out of there."

He called the section he was working on "The Emperor's Somersault." It involved yet another apostasy—the apostasy of a god, which is how Kenzaburo characterizes the emperor's announcement that he was no longer to be considered divine, after Japan's defeat in World War II. The impersonal significance of this god's apostasy is obvious. But so much of Kenzaburo's work has dwelt on this traumatic announcement, and his bitterness against the emperor system has always been so intense—and so personal— that it is tempting to speculate that his sense of the country's betrayal, or desertion, by a kind of ultimate father figure was emotionally fueled by his father's death in the previous year, and that his sense of having been abandoned as a vulnerable child has also been the emotional source of the intensity of his involvement with his own perpetually dependent son.

On May 21, Kenzaburo left Princeton for New York City, to be inducted into the American Academy of Arts and Letters, as Foreign Member. He was going to fly back to Japan the following morning. After the ceremony, he spoke of his dread of resuming a celebrity's life there: "Everyone knows where I live now. Journalists are always coming. Sometimes there are groups of demonstrators, or just tourists who want to take photographs of our house. At least nobody knows our phone number now. But once I get back, I think we're going to have problems with people coming to our house, and I am anxious about it. Hikari doesn't really care. He doesn't have to talk to journalists much, and the number of friends who come to visit him is very small." Someone remarked that he would surely be glad to be with Hikari again. And Kenzaburo's urbane manner changed strikingly. He stared wildly at the questioner, his expression almost desperate, and he heaved a deep sigh. "My God, *yes!*" he said finally, so loudly he was almost shouting. His impatience to resume the jointly creative existence he enjoys with his son had nearly overpowered him.

Bibliography/Discography

Hikari Oe Recordings

Oe, Hikari. *Music of Hikari Oe*. Artists: Akiko Ebi (piano), Hiroshi Koizumi (flute). Denon CO-78952. Recorded 1992.

―――. *Music of Hikari Oe 2*. Artists: Akiko Ebi (piano), Hiroshi Koizumi (flute), Tomoko Kato (violin). Denon CO-78953. Recorded 1994.

Hikari Oe Scores

The Music of Oe Hikari. 5.20.1993. Zenon Gakufu Shuppansha, Higashi Gokencho, 13–14 Shinjuku-ku. Tokyo 162, Japan.

Oe Hikari Again. 10.20.1994. Published by Zenon Gakufu Shuppansha (address as above).

(These scores may be ordered from the publisher.)

Kenzaburo Oe in Translation

Oe, Kenzaburo. "The Clever Rain Tree," trans. Brett de Bary and Carolyn Haynes. In *The Showa Anthology*, eds., Van C. Gessel and Tomone Matsumoto. Tokyo: Kodansha, 1985.

―――. *An Echo of Heaven*, trans. Margaret Mitsutani. Tokyo: Kodansha, 1996.

―――. *A Healing Family*, trans. Stephen Snyder. Tokyo: Kodansha, 1996.

―――. *Hiroshima Notes*, trans. David L. Swain and Toshi Yonezawa. New York/London: Marion Boyars, 1995.

―――. *Japan, the Ambiguous, and Myself*, trans. Kunioki Yanagishita and Hisaaki Yamanouchi. Tokyo: Kodansha, 1995.

―――. *M/T et l'histoire des merveilles de la forêt*, trans. René de Ceccatty and Ryoji Nakamura. Paris: Gallimard, 1989.

―――. "A Mythical Topos" [with John Nathan], *Grand Street* 55 (14:3, 1996).

―――. *Nip the Buds, Shoot the Kids*, trans. Paul St. John Mackintosh and Maki Sugiyama. New York/London: Marion Boyars, 1995.

―――. *A Personal Matter*, trans. John Nathan. New York: Grove, 1969.

―――. *The Pinch Runner Memorandum*, trans. Michiko N. Wilson and Michael K. Wilson. Armonk: M.E. Sharpe, 1994.

―――. *A Quiet Life*, trans. Kunioki Yanagishita and William Wetherall. New York: Grove, 1996.

―――. *Rise Up, O Young Men of the New Age*, trans. John Nathan. New York: Grove (in press).

―――. *Seventeen & J*, trans. Luk Van Haute. New York: Blue Moon, 1996.

————. *The Silent Cry,* trans. John Bester. Tokyo: Kodansha, 1974.

————. *Teach Us to Outgrow Our Madness,* trans. John Nathan. New York: Grove, 1977.

————. "Wave Patterns: A Dialogue" [with Kazuo Ishiguro], *Grand Street* 38 (10:2, 1991).

————. "The Way of Eating Fried Sausage," trans. Mari Hoashi and Masao Miyoshi. *Grand Street* 38. (10:2, 1991).

About Savants

Howe, Michael J. A. *Fragments of Genius: The Strange Feats of Idiots Savants.* London: Routledge, 1989.

Miller, Leon K. *Musical Savants: Exceptional Skill in the Mentally Retarded.* Hillsdale, N.J.: Lawrence Erlbaum, 1989.

Sacks, Oliver. *An Anthropologist on Mars.* New York: Knopf, 1995.

Treffert, Darold A. *Extraordinary People: Understanding "Idiot Savants."* New York: Harper & Row, 1989.

About Kenzaburo Oe

Napier, Susan J. *Escape from the Wasteland: Romanticism and Realism in the Fiction of Mishima Yukio and Oe Kenzaburo.* Cambridge, Mass.: Harvard University Press, 1991.

Wilson, Michiko Niikuni. *The Marginal World of Oe Kenzaburo.* Armonk, N.Y.: M.E. Sharpe, 1986.

Index of Works by Hikari Oe

Index of Works by Kenzaburo Oe